W9-AOD-654

DECORATING
with FABRIC &
WALLCOVERING

98 Projects & Ideas

The Home Decorating Institute®

CREATIVE
PUBLISHING
international

Library of Congress Cataloging-in-Publication Data Decorating with fabric & wallcovering / The Home Decorating Institute. p. cm. — (Arts & crafts
for home decorating) Includes index. ISBN 0-86573-371-6 — ISBN 0-86573-372-4 (pbk.) 1. House furnishings 2. Textile fabrics in interior
decoration. 3. Wall coverings. 4. Interior decoration—Amateurs' manuals. I. Home Decorating Institute (Minnetonka, Minn.) II. Creative Publishing
international, Inc. III. Title: Decorating with fabric and wallcovering IV. Series.   TL387.D44 1995 747'.9 — dc20   94-36572

CONTENTS

Wall Treatments

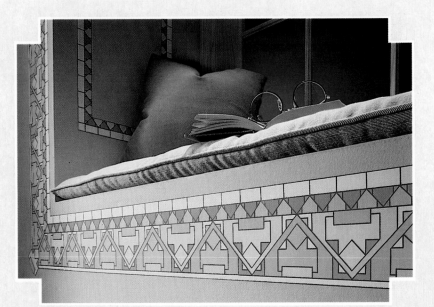

Window Treatments

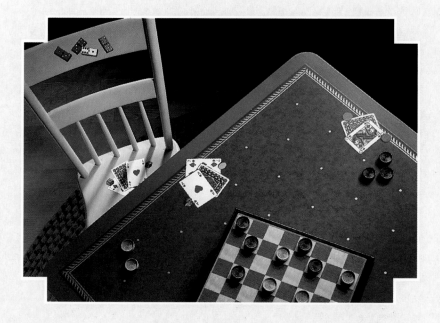

Furniture

Room Accessories

DECORATING WITH FABRIC & WALLCOVERING

Customize your decorating scheme with fabric and wallcovering, making a variety of wall treatments and accessories. Add interest to the walls by using wallcovering in creative ways. Or upholster a wall with fabric for a custom look.

Select from simple window treatments, including tent-flap curtains, swags, and tab curtains. Or use a wallcovering border to make a decorative cornice.

Furnishings, such as screens, headboards, and lamp shades, can be covered with fabric or wallcovering to add pattern or texture to a room. To achieve a trompe l'oeil effect, apply wallcovering designs to a cabinet or chest. Use slipcovers for a quick change on kitchen and dining-room chairs, and make tailored table covers for a variety of tables. Create a button-tufted cushion, a tie-tab pillow, or a fabric-covered picture frame to coordinate the entire room.

*Wall
Treatments*

WALLCOVERING BASICS

Wallcoverings may be used in many creative ways to add interest and variety to a decorating scheme. Wallcoverings with different patterns may be combined to achieve unique effects. To find wallcoverings that work well together, look for patterns that have similar colors or design motifs rather than limiting yourself to patterns that are designed as coordinates.

After selecting a wallcovering, consult the salesperson about the proper adhesive. Many wallcoverings are prepasted and do not need additional adhesive. The paste on these wallcoverings is activated by dipping the wallcovering in water. Unpasted wallcoverings are applied using a clear vinyl adhesive. Border adhesive is often recommended for applying a vinyl border over a vinyl wallcovering; any excess border adhesive must be removed immediately, because it is impossible to remove after it has dried. Some wallcovering pastes may discolor painted surfaces and touching up may be required.

Before applying a wallcovering, clean the wall surface to remove any grease or soil. A solution of equal parts of ammonia and water works well. Repair any cracks or dents by filling them with spackling compound.

For some wallcovering applications, premixed sizing is recommended. This product prevents the adhesive from soaking into the wall surface. It also improves adhesion of the wallcovering and makes it easier to reposition, if necessary. Sizing is recommended for applications in humid areas. Once applied, sizing may be difficult to remove.

Wallcovering tools include a smoothing brush (**a**), a tray for use with prepasted wallcovering (**b**), a carpenter's level (**c**), a natural sea sponge (**d**), a paint tray (**e**), a razor knife with a breakaway blade (**f**), a wide broadknife (**g**), a paint roller (**h**), a seam roller (**i**), and a paste brush (**j**) for applying adhesive to unpasted wallcovering.

HOW TO PREPARE WALLCOVERING

1 **Prepasted wallcovering.** Fill the water tray half full of lukewarm water. Roll cut strip loosely, adhesive side out. Wet the roll in tray as directed by the manufacturer, usually for about 1 minute or less.

2 Hold one edge of the strip with both hands, and lift the wallcovering from the water; check pasted side to make sure strip is evenly wet.

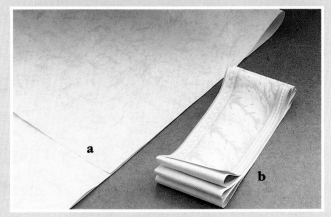

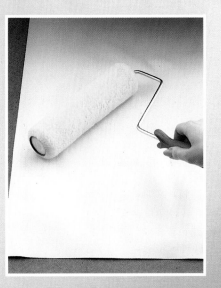

3 Cure short or vertical wallcovering strips by folding ends to center, pasted side in, without creasing folds (**a**); for long horizontal strips, fold the wallcovering strips accordion-style (**b**). Allow the strip to set for about ten minutes.

Unpasted wallcovering. Place the strip patterned side down on a flat surface. Apply adhesive evenly, using paint roller or paste brush. Wipe adhesive from table before preparing next strip. Cure strip as in step 3.

WALLCOVERING BORDERS

Decorating with wallcovering borders is an easy way to add style to a room. Borders can be used to define a space, highlight architectural features, or add interest by creating new lines.

Available in a variety of designs, borders can be used to complement any decorating style. Designs include florals, geometrics, and architectural patterns. To achieve unique effects, borders can be cut apart or combined with other borders. For best results when using a border to outline or frame features of a room, select a border with a nondirectional print, because directional prints may not be pleasing when hung upside down. Some border designs are available with matching or coordinating corner pieces, which add a distinctive finishing touch. You can also make your own custom corner piece by cutting design motifs from wallcovering or wallcovering borders.

When determining the border placement, consider where the placement will draw the eye and what the placement will do to the proportions of the room. A border placed at the top of the wall draws the eye upward, providing a balance with elements at a lower level. Positioned at the picture rail level, a border visually lowers the ceiling. Consider running the border in a continuous band around doors and windows instead of ending the border when it meets the door and window moldings. For borders used as chair rails, position the center of the border one-third of the distance up from the floor on the wall surface.

When hanging borders, begin in an inconspicuous location. Plan the placement, if possible, so the more conspicuous corners are mitered evenly; corners at eye level or higher are usually more noticeable than lower corners. Where the last border segment meets the first, a mismatch usually results.

Wallcovering borders are available by the yard (m) or prepackaged in 5-yd. to 7-yd. (4.6 to 6.4 m) spools. To estimate the yardage needed, measure the areas where the border will be applied. Allow extra yardage for matching adjoining spools and for any damage that may have occurred to the ends of the rolls. Also allow at least twice the border width plus 2" (5 cm) for each mitered corner.

HOW TO HANG WALLCOVERING BORDERS

1 Cut first border strip, and prepare strip (page 9). Draw a light pencil line around room at desired height, using a carpenter's level, if positioning the border at location other than ceiling or baseboard.

2 Position the border at least conspicuous corner. Overlap the border around corner of adjacent wall for ½" (1.3 cm). Press border flat along wall with a smoothing brush; have an assistant hold folded portion of border while you apply and brush it.

3 Form a ¼" (6 mm) tuck just beyond each inside corner. Continue to apply border. Cut border at corner, using a sharp razor knife and wide broadknife.

4 Peel back the tucked strip, and smooth strip around the corner. Press the border flat. Apply seam adhesive to lapped seam, if necessary.

5 Overlap border strips so patterns match, if a seam falls in middle of wall. Cut through both layers, using a wide broadknife and a razor knife. Peel back border, and remove cut ends. Press border flat. Roll seam after ½ hour. Rinse adhesive from border, using damp sponge.

6 Trim border at a door or window frame by holding border against outer edge of frame with a wide broadknife and trimming excess with a sharp razor knife.

HOW TO MITER WALLCOVERING BORDERS

1 Apply the horizontal border strips, extending them past the corners a distance greater than width of the border. Apply vertical border strips, overlapping horizontal strips.

2 Cut through both layers at a 45° angle, using a razor knife and a straightedge. Peel back the border; remove ends.

3 Press the border flat. Roll the seam after ½ hour. Rinse adhesive from seam, using a damp sponge.

TIPS FOR DECORATING WITH WALLCOVERING BORDERS

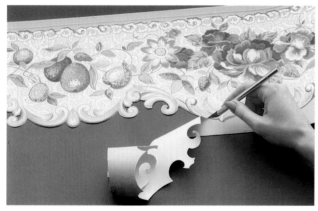

Trim away upper or lower edges of border along lines of design to create interesting effects.

Apply designs cut from borders over mitered corners to camouflage seams.

Make borders economically by cutting standard rolls of wallcovering into border strips. Striped wallcoverings with nondirectional designs are especially suitable.

Finish cut end of border with a length of edging cut from additional length of border. Cut edging strip diagonally at corner to form a mitered appearance with edging on border.

MORE IDEAS FOR WALLCOVERING BORDERS

Combination of borders (above) creates an interesting effect at the ceiling level.

Vertical border strips can be used to divide plain walls. The placement guidelines were marked using a carpenter's level and pencil. An edging strip cut from an additional length of border is used to finish the upper and lower edges. The edging strips are applied to the cut ends of the border as on page 13.

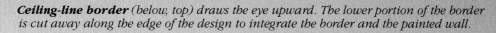

Ceiling-line border *(below, top) draws the eye upward. The lower portion of the border is cut away along the edge of the design to integrate the border and the painted wall.*

Mitered border *(below, bottom) frames a window. Design motifs from the border are cut out and applied over the miters to camouflage the seams.*

WALLCOVERING PANELS

Wallcovering and coordinating borders can be used to create decorative wall panels. The panels are less costly than covering entire rooms and add interest to otherwise plain walls.

Make panels to divide large walls into smaller sections, or use panels to highlight pictures and mirrors. The panels may be identical in size, or wide panels may be alternated with narrow ones. As a general rule, space the panels evenly on the wall, allowing slightly more space between the lower edge of the panel and the baseboard. Begin by planning the placement of the most dominant panels first. You may want to plan placement on graph paper, taking into account the position of any windows, doors, or built-ins. Also take into account any pattern repeat in the wallcovering to allow for matching patterns, if necessary.

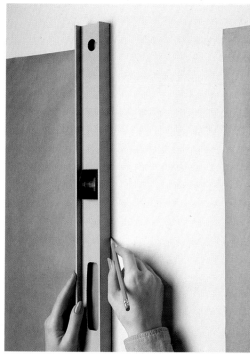

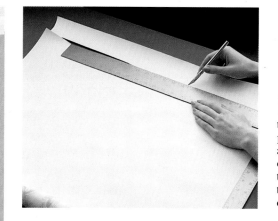

2 Cut a strip of wallcovering for the center of the panel to size, using a framing square to ensure 90° angles at the corners. Prepare the wallcovering as on page 9.

3 Unfold the top portion of the prepared strip. Position lightly on the wall, aligning the wallcovering with marked lines; use your palms to slide the strip in place. Press top of the strip flat with a smoothing brush, checking for bubbles, and reposition as necessary.

1 Determine the size and position of wallcovering panels by cutting and taping paper to the wall. Using a pencil and a carpenter's level, lightly mark the dimensions of the panel on the wall. Measure and record dimensions.

5 Cut and apply any remaining strips, matching pattern and butting seams. Roll seam after ½ hour. Rinse any adhesive from the wallcovering and wall, using clear water and a damp sponge. Prepare border as for unpasted wallcovering (page 9), using border adhesive.

6 Apply border strips to panel in clockwise direction, starting at least conspicuous corner; align outer edge of border with edge of panel and allow ends to extend slightly beyond edges of panel. Miter corners as on page 13, steps 2 and 3; do not affix border firmly at first corner until final border strip is applied. Roll outer edges of border and seams after ½ hour.

4 Unfold bottom of strip; use palms to position strip against marked lines. Press strip flat with smoothing brush, checking for bubbles.

MORE IDEAS FOR WALLCOVERING PANELS

Wall panel creates a border around a painting. Companion corner pieces are used for additional interest.

Ceiling panel (above) draws the eye upward. The placement lines for the panel were determined by measuring in 6" (15 cm) from each wall.

Grouping of panels (below) adds interest to a wall. The square panels near the base of the wall are centered under a long horizontal panel.

WALLCOVERING CUTOUTS

Wallcovering cutouts are design motifs that are cut from wallcovering or borders. The cutout designs can be used to create interesting patterns or trompe l'oeil effects on painted walls. Unique designs can be created by combining motifs from different wallcoverings. For best results, walls should be painted with a high-grade washable paint, such as a low-luster or satin-sheen paint or a flat enamel.

For most wall applications, a clear vinyl adhesive will bond cutouts to the wall surface. If you are applying a border adhesive to prepasted cutouts, it may be desirable to remove the prepasted glue to reduce the thickness of the paper. Remove glue from prepasted wallcovering by soaking the cutout in water and lightly rubbing the pasted side. Blot the cutout with a towel to remove excess water; then apply the desired adhesive.

HOW TO APPLY A WALLCOVERING CUTOUT

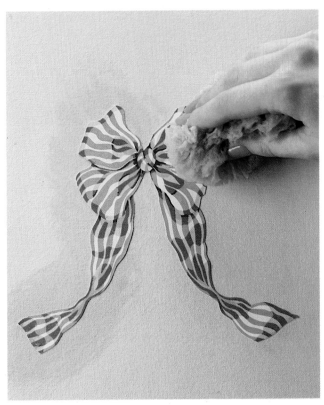

1 Cut wallcovering motifs using a mat knife and cutting surface or a small, sharp scissors; simplify the designs as necessary. For easier handling, make any interior cuts before trimming outer edges.

2 Place the cutout facedown on a sheet of plastic or wax paper. Gently brush on a thin, even layer of adhesive, using a sponge applicator.

3 Press the cutout on surface; smooth out any air bubbles, using damp sponge. Roll the edges firmly with a seam roller. Rinse off any excess adhesive, using damp sponge.

TIPS FOR DECORATING WITH CUTOUTS

Extend length of a motif by cutting it apart and spreading the sections. Fill in the space between sections with smaller designs, such as flowers, rosettes, or bows.

Create a focal point with pictures or plates by using design motifs like ribbons or ropes as faux hangers. Mark position of the picture or plate first, then cut the wallcovering motifs for positioning above and below. The motifs need not continue behind the object.

Plan placement by positioning cutouts temporarily with poster putty. Mark the positions lightly with pencil or use positioned pieces as a guide when securing each motif in place.

MORE IDEAS FOR DECORATING WITH CUTOUTS

Trompe l'oeil embellishes a kitchen wall. Plate, bowl, and vase motifs are cut from a wallcovering border and positioned above a shelf. Apple motifs and an edging strip, cut from a second border, help to unify the look.

Headboard effect is created by positioning cutouts on the wall above the bed.

Floral archway *frames the upper portion of a window, for a feminine look.*

Storybook scene *is created by placing teddy bear motifs in the center of a wallcovering panel (page 16).*

UPHOLSTERED WALLS

Upholstered walls help create an inviting atmosphere. The fabric covers any imperfections on the walls, and the batting used as padding helps insulate the room and absorbs sound. Avoid using fabrics in plaids or stripes, because they call attention to walls that are not squared. Stapling the fabric to drywall or paneled walls is easy; however, staples will not penetrate metal corner pieces. For plaster walls, check to see if staples will penetrate the wall and hold. Before starting, remove switch plates and outlet covers. Do not remove moldings or baseboards, because double welting will cover the fabric edges.

MATERIALS

- Decorator fabric; polyester upholstery batting.
- Staple gun and ⅜" to ½" (1 to 1.3 cm) staples; pushpins; single-edged razor blades; hot glue gun and glue sticks; thick craft glue.

CUTTING DIRECTIONS

Cut fabric lengths as figured in the chart, below; do not trim the selvages unless they show through the fabric. Measure around doors and windows and along the ceiling and baseboard; also measure from the floor to the ceiling at each corner. For the double welting, cut fabric strips, 3" (7.5 cm) wide, equal to the total of these measurements.

WORKSHEET FOR CALCULATING FABRIC

	in. (cm)
Cut Length	
Measurement from floor to ceiling plus 3" (7.5 cm)*	=
Cut Width	
Width of fabric minus selvages	=
Number of Fabric Widths Needed for Each Wall	
Width of wall	=
Divided by cut width of fabric	÷
Number of fabric widths for wall**	=
Amount of Fabric Needed for Double Welting	
Total welting length (see Cutting Directions)	=
Divided by cut width of fabric	÷
Number of strips**	=
Multiplied by 3" (7.5 cm)	×
Fabric needed for double welting	=
Total Fabric Needed	
Cut length (figured above)	=
Number of fabric widths (figured above) for all walls	×
Fabric needed for all walls	=
Fabric needed for double welting	+
Total length needed	=
Divided by 36" (100 cm)	÷
Number of yd. (m) needed	= yd. (m)

Allow extra for pattern repeat; do not subtract for windows and doors unless they cover most of the wall.

**Round up to the nearest whole number.*

HOW TO UPHOLSTER A WALL

1 Staple batting to wall every 6" (15 cm), leaving a 1" (2.5 cm) gap between batting and the edge of ceiling, corners, baseboard, and moldings. Butt edges between widths of batting. Cut out batting around switch and outlet openings.

2 Stitch the fabric panels together for each wall separately, matching pattern (opposite), if necessary. Plan seam placement to avoid seams next to windows and doors. Make double welting (opposite).

3 Start hanging fabric from the top, turning under ½" (1.3 cm) and stapling every 3" to 4" (7.5 to 10 cm). Begin at a corner where matching is not critical. Do not cut around the windows and doors.

4 Anchor fabric in corners, pulling taut and stapling close to corner so the staples will be covered with double welting. Trim excess fabric. Start next panel at corner.

5 Staple along baseboard, pulling and smoothing fabric taut to remove any wrinkles. Trim the excess fabric along baseboard, using single-edged razor blade.

6 Mark outside corners of windows and doors with pushpins. Cut out openings with diagonal cuts into corners. Turn under the raw edges, and staple around the molding.

7 Apply hot glue to the back of double welting, about 5" (12.5 cm) at a time; secure the double welting to the upper and lower edges of wall and around window and door frames. Carefully push the double welting in place to cover the staples.

8 Press double welting into corners and around any openings. Use a screwdriver to push double welting into corners. After glue dries, peel off any excess.

9 Apply fabric to switch plates and outlet covers, securing it with diluted craft glue. Clip and trim around openings. Turn raw edges to back of plate; glue in place.

HOW TO MATCH A PATTERNED FABRIC

1 Position fabric widths, right sides together, matching selvages. Fold back the upper selvage until pattern matches; lightly press foldline.

2 Unfold selvage; pin fabric widths together on foldline. Check match from right side.

3 Repin the fabric widths so pins are perpendicular to the foldline; stitch on the foldline, using a straight stitch. Trim fabric to finished length.

HOW TO MAKE DOUBLE WELTING

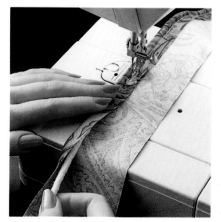

1 Place cording on wrong side of 3" (7.5 cm) fabric strip. Fold the fabric over cording, with ½" (1.3 cm) seam allowance extending. Stitch with the zipper foot next to cording.

2 Place the second cord next to the first cord. Bring the fabric over the second length of cording.

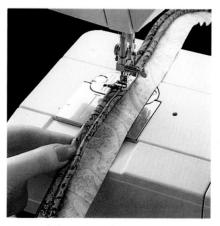

3 Stitch between the two cords on previous stitching line. Trim off excess fabric next to stitching; the raw edge is on the back of finished double welting.

MORE IDEAS FOR FABRICS ON WALLS

Banded fabric panels (left) hang from a peg rail. The panels are made following the directions for tab curtains on pages 46 to 49. One and one-half times fullness was used.

Sheer fabric panels (above) hang from decorative hooks. The panels are made following the directions for tab curtains on pages 46 to 49. Knotted lengths of cording replace the fabric tabs. Two times fullness was used to achieve a draped effect.

Decorator fabric (right) is used to upholster the walls above the chair rail. Braid trim is used instead of double welting.

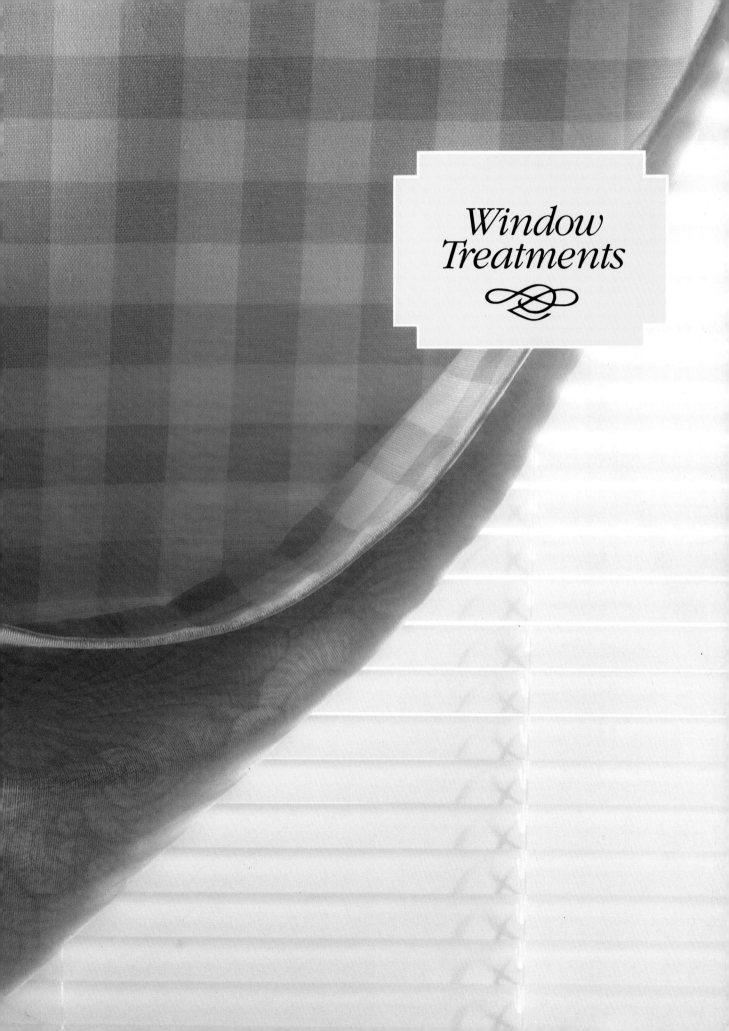

Window
Treatments

TENT-FLAP CURTAINS

Tent-flap curtains add an uncluttered, stylish look to windows. Depending on the fabric choice and the draping of the flaps, tent-flap curtains can be tailored or unstructured in style. These curtains work especially well on small windows.

The folded flaps of the curtains can be hand-tacked in place, or they can be secured with a button and buttonhole to allow for opening and closing. The style of the folded flaps may vary with the size of the window. Experiment by folding back the front edges and corners of the panels to determine the most suitable style for a particular window.

Tent-flap curtains are attached to a mounting board and may be mounted either inside or outside the window frame. For an inside mount, use a 1 × 1 mounting board. Cut the mounting board ½" (1.3 cm) shorter than the inside measurement of the window frame; this ensures that the mounting board will fit inside the frame after it is covered with fabric. For an outside mount, use a 1 × 2 mounting board. An outside-mounted board may be mounted either at the top of the window frame or on the wall above the window. Cut the mounting board at least 2" (5 cm) longer than the window frame to allow space for mounting the angle irons. Secure the angle irons to wall studs whenever possible, using pan-head screws. Or use molly bolts if the angle irons do not align with the wall studs.

MATERIALS

- Decorator fabric, for curtains and covered mounting board.
- Matching or contrasting fabric, for lining.
- Mounting board.
- Heavy-duty stapler; staples.
- Angle irons and 8 × ¾" (2 cm) pan-head screws or molly bolts, for outside mount.
- Two 1½" (3.8 cm) lengths of 1 × 2 board and self-adhesive hook and loop tape, for outside mount.
- 8 × 1½" (3.8 cm) pan-head screws, for inside mount.
- Two cup hooks and two small rings, for inside mount.

CUTTING DIRECTIONS

The cut length of each curtain panel is equal to the desired finished length plus the depth of the mounting board plus 1" (2.5 cm) for ½" (1.3 cm) seam allowances. The cut width of each panel is equal to one-half the width of the mounting board plus 2" (5 cm) to allow for seam allowances and 1" (2.5 cm) overlap. For outside-mounted curtains, also add the depth, or projection, of the mounting board. Cut two panels each, from fabric and lining, to this length and width.

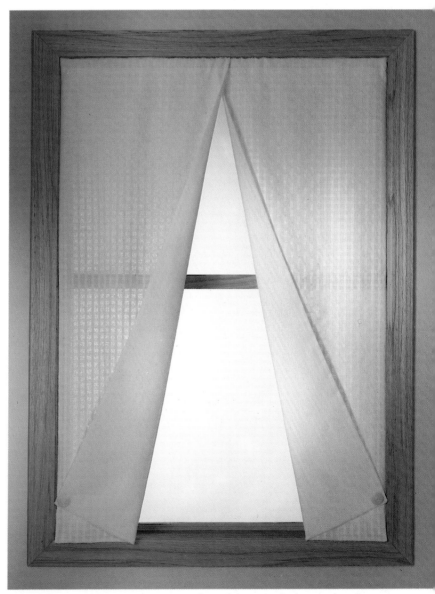

Tent-flap curtains may be mounted inside or outside the window frame. Above, inside-mounted curtains are constructed from two sheer fabrics. Opposite, outside-mounted curtains made from decorator fabric have a contrasting lining fabric for a coordinated look.

1 Cut fabric to cover the mounting board, with width of fabric equal to distance around board plus 1" (2.5 cm) and length of fabric equal to length of board plus 3½" (9 cm). Center board on wrong side of fabric. Fold one long edge of fabric over board.

2 Staple the edge of the fabric to board, placing the staples about 8" (20.5 cm) apart; do not staple within 6" (15 cm) of ends. Wrap fabric around the board; fold under ⅜" (1 cm) on long edge, and staple to board, placing staples about 6" (15 cm) apart.

3 Miter fabric at corners on side of board with unfolded edge of fabric; finger-press. Staple miters in place near the raw edge.

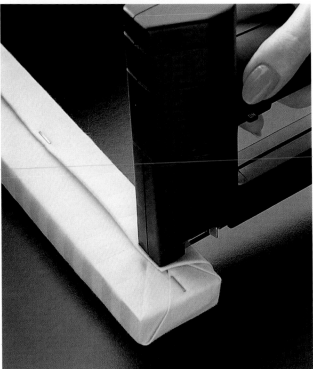

4 Miter fabric at corners on side of board with folded fabric edge; finger-press. Fold under excess fabric at ends; staple near fold. Set aside covered board until step 8.

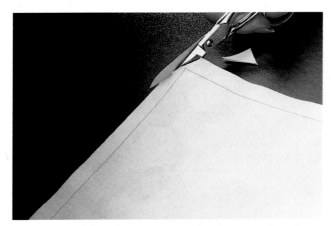

5 Pin outer fabric for curtain panel to lining, right sides together, matching the raw edges. Stitch ½" (1.3 cm) seams around all sides; leave 8" (20.5 cm) opening at the center of upper edge for turning. Trim corners diagonally.

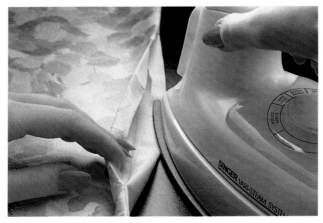

6 Press seam allowances open. Trim seams, if necessary. Turn panel right side out. Press edges, pressing in seam allowances at center opening.

7 Stitch horizontal buttonhole at the inside edge of each panel or diagonal buttonholes at the lower inside corner, if desired.

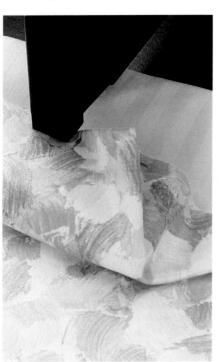

8 Staple panels to the board, aligning upper edge of panels to back edge of board; at corner, make diagonal fold to form a miter. Panels will overlap 1" (2.5 cm) at the center.

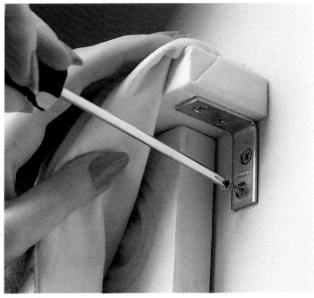

9 Secure angle irons to the bottom of mounting board, near ends, using pan-head screws. Secure angle irons to top of window frame or to wall, using pan-head screws or molly bolts.

(Continued)

10 Fold the corner or front edge of each panel back to the outer edges as desired; pin in place, making sure sides are even. Attach button to use with buttonhole, or hand-tack the layers together and embellish with decorative button.

11 Cut 1½" (3.8 cm) length from excess mounting board for the projection on each side of window. Mount one block of wood on each side of window frame, at about the height of button placement, using angle irons. Secure the lining to wood with small piece of self-adhesive hook and loop tape.

HOW TO SEW INSIDE-MOUNTED TENT-FLAP CURTAINS

1 Follow steps 1 to 7 on pages 34 and 35; staple panels on mounting board, overlapping them 1" (2.5 cm) so they are centered on board. Panels may extend slightly beyond the ends of the board.

2 Mount curtain by securing board inside of window frame, using 8 × 1½" (3.8 cm) pan-head screws; predrill the holes, using ⅛" drill bit.

3 Stitch small ring to curtain lining at lower outside edge. Position a cup hook inside frame, and secure. Attach ring to hook. Complete the curtains as in step 10, above.

MORE IDEAS FOR TENT-FLAP CURTAINS

Draped tent-flap curtains *have a relaxed look. The soft draping is achieved by fastening the corners of the panels near the top of the curtain. Buttons and fabric button loops are used to fasten the flaps.*

Lace and sheer fabric *make tent-flap curtains that filter sunlight. Ribbon bows are tacked to the front of the flaps for embellishment.*

Single flap *is secured to the front of an inside-mounted board, using buttons and buttonholes. Buttons are stitched to the fabric-covered mounting board, and buttonholes are stitched at the upper edge of the fabric panel.*

TAILORED SWAGS

This simple swag is created by mounting a fabric panel to a board and using fabric tabs on each end to hold the swagged fabric in place. The tailored look is achieved by fan folding the fabric panel before mounting it to the board. The fabric at the ends of the panel drapes to form jabots, or side panels. These jabots can be cut straight or tapered at the lower edge. Use this top treatment alone or with blinds, pleated shades, or sheer curtain panels.

This swag works best as an outside mount, positioned about 2" to 3" (5 to 7.5 cm) above the woodwork. If the board is mounted higher, be sure to make the tabs that support the swags long enough to conceal the woodwork. Mount the swag on a 1 × 3 board if there is no undertreatment. With an undertreatment, use a mounting board that will project out from the window frame far enough for the swag to clear the undertreatment by 1" to 2" (2.5 to 5 cm). The length of the mounting board is equal to the desired finished width of the top treatment. Cut the board at least 1" (2.5 cm) wider than the window frame.

The length of the jabots should be in proportion to the overall width and look of the window. As a general rule, the jabots should end slightly above or below the middle of the window.

Select a fabric that has a nondirectional print so the lengthwise grain of the fabric can be run horizontally across the width of the window. This allows the swag to be constructed without piecing.

CUTTING DIRECTIONS

Use the full width of the fabric. Determine the cut length of the panel by measuring the desired finished length of each jabot and the length of the mounting board; add 1" (2.5 cm) for seam allowances. Cut the fabric and lining to this length.

For each tab, cut one fabric strip with a width of 6" (15 cm) and a length of about 28" (71 cm).

HOW TO MAKE A TAILORED SWAG

MATERIALS

- Decorator fabric.
- Lining, in same width as outer fabric.
- Mounting board.
- Staple gun and staples.
- Angle irons and pan-head screws or molly bolts.

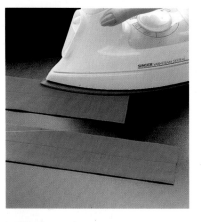

1 Trim selvages from the outer fabric. For jabots with tapered lower edges, pin-mark 12" to 18" (30.5 to 46 cm) from corners at lower edge of fabric. Draw diagonal lines from pin marks to corners at upper edge. Cut on marked lines. Cut lining to same size, using outer fabric as a guide for cutting tapered edges.

2 Pin outer fabric to the lining, right sides together. Stitch ½" (1.3 cm) seam around all sides, leaving 12" (30.5 cm) opening at center of upper edge for turning. Trim the corners diagonally. Press the seams open. Turn right side out. Press edges, folding in seam allowances at center opening.

3 Fold tab strip in half, lengthwise; stitch ½" (1.3 cm) seam. Repeat for the remaining tab. Turn tabs right side out; press, with seam centered on the back side.

4 Cover mounting board as on page 34, steps 1 to 4. Staple one tab, seam side up, to mounting board, with the raw edge centered and the pressed edge about ¼" (6 mm) from one end of the board. Repeat at opposite end.

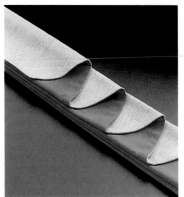

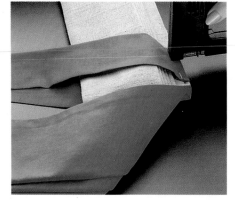

5 Place the fabric right side up. Fan-fold the entire width of the panel in about 4" (10 cm) folds, beginning at side opposite the longest edge.

6 Center folded panel on the mounting board, aligning longest edge to back edge of board; staple in place. Pull tab around to the front and adjust to desired position; turn under the raw edge of the tab and staple to board. Repeat for the remaining tab.

7 Mount swag as on page 35, step 9. Tug gently on lower edge of center swagged portion to achieve desired look. Adjust tabs and arrange folds in swag and jabots; separate outer fabric and lining, if desired, for a fuller swag.

MORE IDEAS FOR TAILORED SWAGS

Braid trim *(above) is used in place of fabric tabs to hold the swag in place.*

Grosgrain ribbon *(left) is stitched to the lower edge of the swag and jabots for contrast.*

Fabric bows *(below) are stitched to the tabs for a romantic touch.*

SHIRRED SWAGS

Less formal than a traditional swag, this lined, pole-mounted swag is easy to make. Shirring tape, stitched to a straight fabric panel, creates the swag with jabots, or side panels. The jabots on this treatment hang in a loose, unstructured style and are stapled in place to conceal the shirring. Welting, inserted at the edges of the swag, adds a finishing touch.

Mount the swag 2" to 3" (5 to 7.5 cm) above the window frame to avoid covering too much of the window. The instructions that follow are for jabots approximately 28" (71 cm) long at the longest point; this length may vary, depending on the amount of shirring.

For best results, select a fabric with a nondirectional print, so that the lengthwise grain of the fabric can be run horizontally across the width of the window. This allows the swag to be constructed without piecing fabric widths together.

MATERIALS

- Decorator fabric.
- Lining.
- 2½ yd. (2.3 m) two-cord shirring tape that gathers to at least four times fullness.
- 5⁄32" (3.8 mm) cording, for welting.
- Wood pole, finials, and keyhole support brackets.

CUTTING DIRECTIONS

Determine the cut length of the fabric panel by measuring the length of the mounting pole and adding 49" (125 cm) to this measurement for the jabots and seam allowances. Cut the fabric and the lining to this length. Trim the outer fabric and the lining to 44" (112 cm) in width. For the welting, cut bias fabric strips 1⅝" (4 cm) wide; piece lengths together as necessary for the measurement determined for the cording in step 1, below.

HOW TO MAKE A SHIRRED SWAG

1 Measure pole length. Center and pin-mark this distance on upper edge of rectangle cut from outer fabric. Measure remaining distance around rectangle, from pin mark to pin mark; cut cording for welting to this measurement plus 1" (2.5 cm). Make welting as on page 90, step 1.

2 Pin welting to right side of outer fabric, matching raw edges and extending ends of welting ½" (1.3 cm) beyond pin marks; clip the welting at the corners. Remove the stitching from the welting for ½" (1.3 cm) at the ends; remove cording up to pin mark.

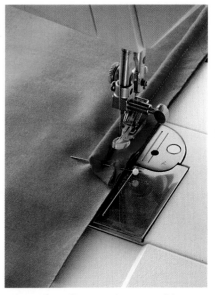

3 Stitch welting to the outer fabric, using zipper foot; fold over ½" (1.3 cm) of welting fabric at ends.

(Continued)

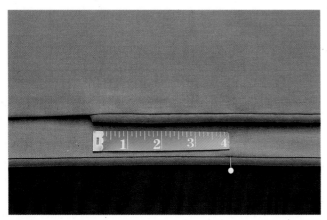

4 Pin lining and outer fabric right sides together; stitch around all four sides close to the previous stitching, leaving a 12" (30.5 cm) opening at center of upper edge. Trim corners diagonally; turn right side out. Press, folding in seam allowances at center opening. Fold panel in half, aligning upper and lower edges; pin-mark lower edge of panel on lining 4" (10 cm) out from end of welting.

5 Position shirring tape diagonally on lining from end of welting to pin mark on lower edge of panel; turn under 1" (2.5 cm) at ends. Use pin to pull out cords. Stitch tape next to cords, through all layers.

6 Knot cords at upper edge of panel; at lower edge, pull evenly on the cords to shirr fabric. Tie off, leaving long tails.

7 Hold pole firmly against the table; using pencil, draw a line on pole where it touches the table.

8 Center the swag on pole, aligning upper edge to marked line on pole; staple in place.

9 Pinch jabot fabric 2" to 4" (5 to 10 cm) from upper edge; pull fabric up to pole and staple in place, concealing shirring tape. Secure the finials to pole.

10 Install pole. Adjust length of shirring, if desired; cut off excess cord length.

Multicolored rope trim *is draped through the swag and hangs over the jabots on each side.*

Twisted welting *is used instead of fabric welting for added textural interest.*

Scalloped loop fringe *is topstitched to the outer edges of this swag for visual impact.*

TAB CURTAINS

Versatile tab curtains offer a variety of looks with either long or short tabs. The unlined panels are constructed with a facing at the upper edge. If desired, the facing can be cut from contrasting fabric and folded to the front of the panel for a banded effect. The facing strip should have a finished width of 1" (2.5 cm) or wider if a contrasting band is desired.

Hang the curtains from a decorative pole set, or for a unique look, hang them from decorative knobs inserted into the woodwork above the window. The pole set may be mounted on or above the window frame, depending on the desired look.

Decorative knobs are available in many styles and finishes. Some styles include screws suitable for inserting into the woodwork. Other knobs, intended for use with a bolt, can be secured to woodwork using hanger bolts (page 48). These bolts, available at specialty woodworking stores, have a metal thread at one end for inserting them into the knob, and a wood thread at the opposite end for inserting into the woodwork. Knobs are generally mounted 4" to 10" (10 to 25.5 cm) apart, depending on the size of the window and the amount of drape desired. To avoid splitting the woodwork, predrill holes before inserting the knobs.

Tab curtains can be designed for a variety of looks. The tab curtains above have a coordinating band at the upper edge and are mounted on a pole set. The tab curtain opposite hangs from decorative knobs and is pulled to the side with a length of cording.

HOW TO DETERMINE THE TAB LENGTH

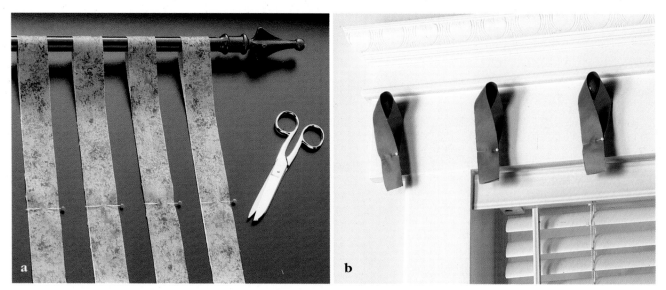

Determine the tab length by pinning fabric strips over pole or rod **(a)** or around knob **(b);** mark tab at the desired distance, using pins. The tabs may be 4" to 8" (10 to 20.5 cm) in length.

HOW TO SEW TAB CURTAINS

MATERIALS

- Lightweight to mediumweight decorator fabric.
- Decorative pole set or knobs.
- Hanger bolts, if necessary, for securing knobs to woodwork.

Decorative knobs that have screws with a wood thread at one end are suitable for inserting into woodwork. Knobs that have screws without a wood thread **(a)** can be made suitable for inserting into woodwork by replacing the screw with a hanger bolt **(b).** Hanger bolts have a metal thread at one end for inserting into the knob and a wood thread at the opposite end for inserting into the woodwork.

CUTTING DIRECTIONS

Determine the desired finished length of the curtain by measuring from the bottom of the pole or knob to the desired finished hem; then subtract the amount of space, or distance, desired between the lower edge of the pole or knob and the upper edge of the curtain.

The cut length of the curtain is equal to the desired finished length of the curtain plus 2½" (6.5 cm) to allow for a 1" (2.5 cm) double-fold hem at the lower edge and a ½" (1.3 cm) seam allowance at the upper edge.

The cut width of the curtain is equal to one and one-half to two times the length of the pole or width of the window. If you are sewing two curtain panels, divide this measurement by two to determine the cut width of each panel. For each panel, add 4" (10 cm) to allow for 1" (2.5 cm) double-fold side hems. If it is necessary to piece fabric widths together to make each panel, also add 1" (2.5 cm) for each seam.

Determine the spacing and the number of tabs for each curtain panel. The tabs are spaced from 6" to 12" (15 to 30.5 cm) apart, depending on the amount of fullness or drape desired between the tabs. Determine the tab length (above). Cut two 1¼" (3.2 cm) strips of fabric for each tab to the determined measurement, adding ½" (1.3 cm) at each end for seam allowances.

Cut the facing strip twice the desired width plus 1" (2.5 cm) for seam allowances. The cut length of the facing strip is equal to the cut width of the panel; piece strips together as necessary for the desired length.

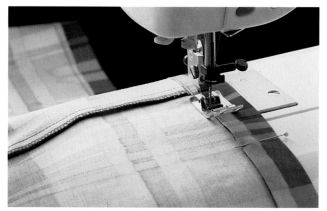

1 Stitch fabric widths together for each panel, stitching ½" (1.3 cm) seams. Finish the seams. At lower edge of the panel, press under 1" (2.5 cm) twice to wrong side of panel; stitch, using straight stitch or blindstitch, to make double-fold hem.

2 Place two tab strips right sides together, matching raw edges. Stitch ¼" (6 mm) seam on long edges. Repeat for remaining tabs. Turn tabs right side out, and press.

3 Fold tabs in half as shown opposite for knob or pole mount. Pin to upper edge of curtain panel, matching raw edges. Pin tabs to right side of panel if facing will be folded to wrong side; pin tabs to wrong side of panel if facing will be folded to the right side for contrasting band. Place tabs at ends 2" (5 cm) from each side; space remaining tabs evenly between the end tabs. Machine-baste tabs in place.

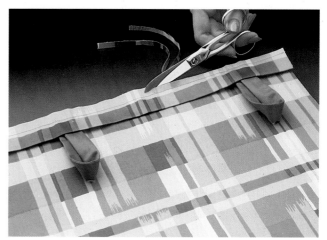

4 Fold the facing strip in half lengthwise, wrong sides together; press. Pin the facing to right side of panel at upper edge, matching raw edges; or, for contrasting band, pin to wrong side of panel. Stitch ½" (1.3 cm) seam at upper edge; trim to ¼" (6 mm).

5 Press the facing to wrong side of panel; or, for contrasting band, press the band to right side. Topstitch close to upper edge and folded edge of facing or band.

6 Press under 1" (2.5 cm) twice at the sides. Stitch to make double-fold hems, using a straight stitch or blindstitch.

7 Hang the curtain panel from knobs or from a decorative pole set.

CORNICES

Use wallcovering borders to create sleek, tailored cornices. These cornices are especially attractive when used with simple undertreatments, such as shades, blinds, and sheer curtain panels. For a finished look, paint the edges of the cornice to match or coordinate with the edge of the wallcovering border.

Determine the inside measurements for the cornice only after any undertreatment is in place. The cornice should clear the undertreatment by 2" to 3" (5 to 7.5 cm), and it should extend at least 2" (5 cm) beyond the end brackets for the rod on each side. Choose a wallcovering border that is wide enough for the completed cornice to cover any drapery heading and hardware.

MATERIALS

- ½" (3.8 cm) finish plywood with smooth finish on at least one side.
- Wallcovering border; border adhesive; sponge applicator.
- Wood glue; wood filler; medium-grit sandpaper.
- 16 × 1½" (3.8 cm) brads; nail set.
- Primer suitable for paint and wallcovering.
- Paint to coordinate with or match the edge of the wallcovering border.
- Angle irons; pan-head screws or molly bolts.

CUTTING DIRECTIONS

Measure and cut the plywood for the top piece of the cornice to correspond to the inside measurements of the cornice, as necessary for the clearance of the undertreatment. Cut the cornice front piece to the expanded width of the wallcovering border (below). The cut width of the cornice front is equal to the width of the cornice top plus two times the thickness of the plywood. Cut the cornice side pieces equal to the expanded width of the wallcovering border by the depth of the cornice top.

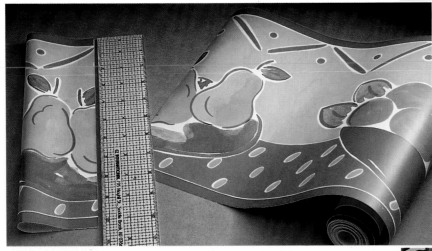

Determine the expanded width of the wallcovering border by applying border adhesive to a 6" (15 cm) length of border. Fold the border in half; allow to set about 5 minutes, then remeasure the width. This is the actual height to cut the cornice front and side pieces.

HOW TO MAKE A CORNICE

1 Glue and nail each side piece to the top piece, aligning upper edges; secure with nails. Glue and nail the front piece, aligning it to the top and side pieces.

2 Countersink nails. Fill nail holes with wood filler; fill front, sides, and lower edges of plywood as necessary. Sand front and side surfaces and edges smooth.

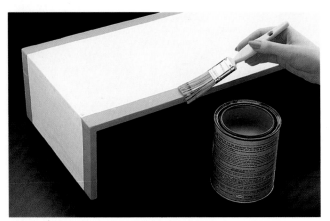

3 Apply primer; allow to dry. Paint lower edges and top of the cornice, extending paint slightly over edges to front and sides; paint inside of cornice.

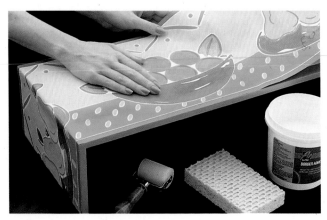

4 Cut wallcovering border equal to distance around the sides and front of the cornice plus 4" (10 cm). Prepare wallcovering as for unpasted wallcovering (page 9), using border adhesive. Center wallcovering on cornice, wrapping wallcovering around the back edge of cornice just to the inside edge of plywood; trim excess paper.

5 Secure angle irons on inside of cornice top, near ends and at 45" (115 cm) intervals or less. Hold cornice at desired placement, making sure it is level; mark the screw holes on wall or window frame. Remove angle irons from cornice. Secure angle irons to wall, using pan-head screws drilled into wall studs, or use molly bolts. Reattach the cornice to installed angle irons.

MORE IDEAS FOR CORNICES

Border edging strip, *cut from a companion wallcovering border, trims the upper and lower edges of a shaped cornice.*

Stacked borders *add height to the cornice above.*

Scalloped border *at right is used to create a cornice with a shaped lower edge. The scallops are cut, using a jigsaw with a fine-toothed scroll-cut blade.*

Furniture

HEADBOARDS

Create a custom headboard by securing either fabric or wallcovering to a wooden base. The upholstered headboard is lightly padded and may be either plain or trimmed around the edges with gimp or decorative nails. The headboard with wallcovering is trimmed with corner molding. Additional decorative moldings can be added, if desired. Both styles are wall-mounted with sawtooth hangers, eliminating the need for attaching the headboard to the bed frame.

The width of the headboard is equal to the width of the bed frame plus an allowance for the bedding. The height of the headboard is about 20" to 24" (51 to 61 cm). The base for the upholstered headboard may be shaped at the upper edge. A rectangular base is recommended for the wallcovering headboard, for ease in mitering the corner molding. Make a paper pattern of the headboard, and place it on the wall behind the bed. Check the size and shape, and adjust as necessary. You may also want to locate the wall studs and mark their locations on the pattern.

For best results on upholstered headboards, select textured fabrics, such as tapestries, because these fabrics are easier to work with. Avoid shiny or tightly woven fabrics. When choosing wallcovering, select solid vinyls for the most durability; these will not absorb skin and hair oils. To avoid seams, select a wallcovering that can be applied horizontally.

Upholstered headboard (opposite) is trimmed with gimp.

Wallcovering headboard (below) uses a coordinating border as an accent around the edges.

HOW TO MAKE A WALLCOVERING HEADBOARD

MATERIALS

- ¾" (2 cm) particleboard, cut to shape.
- Wallcovering and wallcovering border.
- Wallcovering primer; border adhesive.
- Wallcovering tools as needed (page 9).
- 1⅛" (2.8 cm) corner molding, for framing headboard.
- Decorative moldings, optional.

- ⅞" (2.2 cm) finishing nails; nail set.
- Miter box and backsaw.
- Paint, or stain and matching putty, for molding.
- Wood glue; fine-grit sandpaper.
- Large sawtooth picture hangers.
- Two 1½" × ¾" (3.8 × 2 cm) corner braces.

1 Apply wallcovering primer to the particleboard; allow to dry. Paint or stain the back side of the particleboard, if desired.

2 Prepare wallcovering as for unpasted wallcovering (page 9), using border adhesive. Apply wallcovering to particleboard, trimming edges even with edge of board. Position molding on upper edge of the headboard; mark inside edge of molding, using pencil. Repeat for sides. Prepare wallcovering border, and apply to upper edges and sides, lapping border ⅛" (3 mm) beyond marked lines; miter corners as on page 13.

3 Miter the corner molding for sides of headboard at upper corners, using backsaw and miter box; leave excess length on the molding strips. Miter one corner on moldings for upper and lower edges of headboard, leaving excess length.

4 Position upper and side molding strips in place. Mark the angle of the cut at finished length of upper piece. Cut on marked line, using backsaw and miter box.

5 Reposition moldings. Mark finished length and angle of cut for each side piece; cut moldings on marked lines.

6 Position lower molding, aligning mitered corner. Mark finished length and angle of cut; cut miter. Reposition the moldings; sand the mitered corners, if necessary, for proper fit.

7 Paint or stain moldings as desired. Apply bead of glue to the molding, and position on the headboard. Use glue to secure mitered ends of moldings. Secure moldings to headboard, using finishing nails; predrill nail holes with 1/16" drill bit.

8 Countersink finishing nails, using nail set. Fill the holes with putty to match the stain, or touch up with paint.

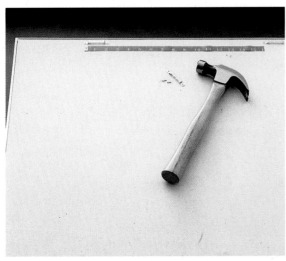

9 Secure two to four sawtooth hangers to the back of the headboard, slotted edge down; position to align with wall stud locations, if possible.

10 Secure corner braces to the lower edge of the headboard, positioning one near each end. Hang headboard on wall, using sawtooth hangers. Secure corner braces to wall. Use molly bolts, if hangers and corner braces do not align with wall studs.

HOW TO MAKE AN UPHOLSTERED HEADBOARD

MATERIALS

- ¾" (2 cm) plywood in AC grade.
- Decorator fabric.
- Lining, such as muslin, for back.
- Polyurethane foam, ½" (1.3 cm) thick and slightly larger than desired size of headboard.
- Polyester upholstery batting.

- Aerosol foam adhesive.
- Heavy-duty stapler; staples.
- Gimp trim; thick craft glue.
- Medium-grit sandpaper.
- Large sawtooth picture hangers.
- Two 1½" × ¾" (3.8 × 2 cm) corner braces.

CUTTING DIRECTIONS

Cut the plywood base to the desired size and shape of the headboard. Cut the decorator fabric and upholstery batting 6" (15 cm) wider and longer than the plywood base. Cut the lining fabric to the size of the plywood base.

1 Sand edges and corners of headboard to round them off slightly.

2 Affix foam to front of headboard, using aerosol foam adhesive; trim the foam even with edges of headboard.

3 Center and affix the batting over the foam, using aerosol foam adhesive; stretch batting slightly.

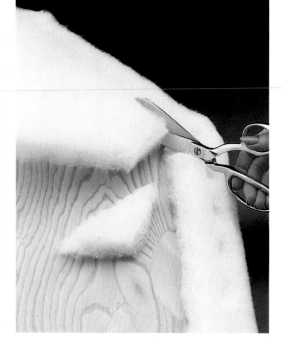

4 Turn the headboard over; wrap the batting to back side. Staple the batting to the plywood about 1" (2.5 cm) from edges; notch inside corners and clip curves, to eliminate bulk. Trim the batting about 1½" (3.8 cm) from edges.

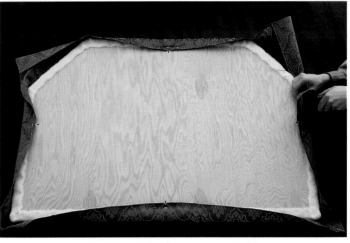

5 Mark center of each side on back of headboard. Notch edge of outer fabric at center of each side. Place the fabric on table, wrong side up. Center the headboard batting side down on fabric.

6 Staple fabric to back of headboard at center of upper edge, about 1½" (3.8 cm) from edge. Stretch the fabric from top to bottom; staple at center of lower edge, matching marks. Repeat at center of each side.

7 Staple the fabric to the back of the headboard at 1½" (3.8 cm) intervals, working from center out, to within 3" (7.5 cm) of corners.

8 Wrap fabric diagonally at corners; staple. Pull the fabric at the sides to the corner; staple. Trim excess fabric.

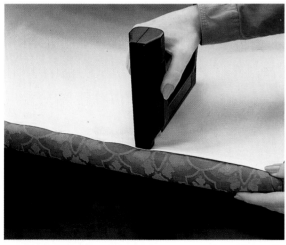

9 Center the lining fabric over back of headboard. Staple in place, folding under raw edges about ½" (1.3 cm); work from the center out, on each side.

10 Apply gimp trim to upper and side edges of the headboard, using thick craft glue. Complete headboard as on page 59, steps 9 and 10.

MORE IDEAS FOR HEADBOARDS

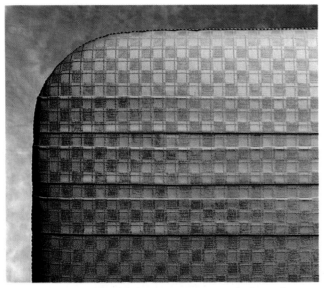

Pleats *add dimension to an upholstered headboard. The pleats are stitched before the fabric is cut to size.*

Wallcovering cutouts *are used as accents on a wallcovering headboard. Apply the cutouts as on pages 20 and 21.*

Wallcovering border *(below) is used horizontally at the upper edge of a headboard. Decorative painted finials are secured on each end of the headboard. Predrill the holes for the finials through the corner molding and particleboard.*

Covered buttons (above), spaced about 8" (20.5 cm) apart, accent a headboard with rounded upper corners. Drill the holes in the headboard and secure the buttons as on pages 72 and 73.

Angular headboard (below) is upholstered with tapestry fabric and embellished along the edges with closely spaced decorative nails in an antiqued brass finish.

FOLDING SCREENS

A decorative folding screen adds impact to a room and can be used to balance the room's proportions. Screens can also serve as dividers in large rooms or multipurpose rooms. These folding screens, covered with fabric or wallcoverings, are made using hollow-core interior doors. Hollow-core doors provide a lightweight, but stable, base and resist warping. If desired, the doors can be shortened as on page 69. Double-action hinges allow the screen panels to swing in both directions.

Fabric-covered screens are lightly padded with a thin layer of foam, then wrapped with fabric. The edges of the doors are covered with a coordinating braid or ribbon to conceal the staples and the raw edges of the fabric.

For a screen covered with wallcovering, the wallcovering can be applied to just the front of the screen, or to both the front and back. The edges of the doors are painted to coordinate with the front and back of the screen.

Decorative screen *can add interest to a room, in addition to serving as a privacy divider. The screen opposite uses a fabric with an all-over floral pattern for the center panel and a striped coordinate for each of the side panels. On the folding screen at right, wallcovering is applied to the entire surface of the panels. The hot air balloons are cutouts from a companion wallcovering.*

HOW TO COVER A FOLDING SCREEN WITH FABRIC

MATERIALS

- Decorator fabric.

- Three hollow-core interior doors, 18" × 80" × 1⅜" (46 × 203.5 × 3.5 cm).

- Flat trim, such as grosgrain ribbon or braid.

- ¼" (6 mm) polyurethane foam.

- Aerosol foam adhesive.

- Thick craft glue.

- Heavy-duty stapler (electric stapler is recommended) and ⅜" (1 cm) staples.

- Six double-action hinges, 1⅛" × 2" (2.8 × 5 cm), with screws.

- Six 1" (2.5 cm) glides.

- Drill and drill bit; size of drill bit depends on size of screws for hinges.

1 Cut foam about 2" (5 cm) larger than dimensions of door. Apply thin, even layer of aerosol foam adhesive to front of door and to one side of foam. Center foam on door; press lightly to secure.

2 Trim the foam even with the edges of the door, using scissors. Continue to apply the foam to both sides of each door.

3 Lay fabric on work surface, wrong side up. Position door on fabric, with the length of door on lengthwise grain of fabric; center any design motifs. Trim fabric 3" (7.5 cm) from edges of door.

4 Wrap the fabric around one side of door, starting at center of one long edge; staple just beyond center of the door edge to anchor fabric. Repeat on the opposite side of the door. Staple fabric along one long edge of door, at 2" (5 cm) intervals, working from center out and keeping grainline of fabric straight.

5 Trim the excess fabric close to the staples.

6 Turn door over. Staple fabric along opposite side of the door; work from the center out, smoothing fabric and pulling taut. If fabric is pulled too tightly, indentations may occur along the edge of the door. Trim excess fabric close to the staples.

7 Wrap the fabric around corners at upper edge of the door; staple. Wrap fabric over upper edge of door, mitering the fabric at corners; secure with staples at 2" (5 cm) intervals, working from center out. Trim excess fabric close to staples. Repeat at lower edge of door.

8 Repeat steps 3 to 7, to cover other side of door. Cover remaining doors.

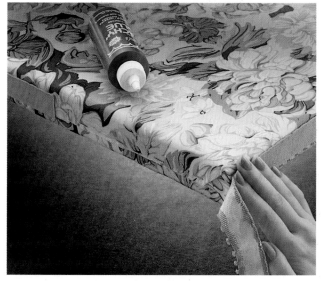

9 Apply flat trim to edges of door, using craft glue and starting at lower edge; butt trim at ends.

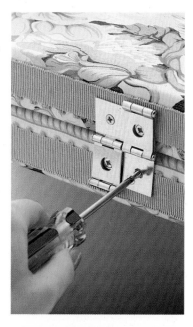

10 Position the middle door on one outer door, aligning all edges. Place open hinge along side edges of the doors at center, with center of hinge between the doors. Mark placement of screws on doors. Mark placement for second and third hinges about 10" (25 cm) from the upper and lower edges of doors. Predrill the holes; attach hinges.

11 Position remaining outer door on the middle door. Attach three hinges to the side edges of these doors on side opposite the previously attached hinges.

12 Tap the glides into the bottom of the doors near each end.

HOW TO COVER A FOLDING SCREEN WITH WALLCOVERING

MATERIALS

- Three hollow-core interior doors, 18" × 80" × 1⅜" (46 × 203.5 × 3.5 cm).
- Wallcovering.
- Primer, suitable for paint and wallcovering.

- Border adhesive.
- Paint to coordinate with wallcovering.
- Paintbrush.
- Wallcovering tools as needed (page 9).

- Six double-action hinges, 1⅛" × 2" (2.8 × 5 cm), with screws.
- Six 1" (2.5 cm) glides.
- Drill and drill bit; size of drill bit depends on size of screws for hinges.

1 Apply primer to doors. Paint side edges of doors, extending paint about ½" (1.3 cm) around edges to front and back. Paint back of door, if wallcovering will be applied to the front only. Apply second coat of paint, if necessary.

2 Cut wallcovering to dimensions of door; use framing square to ensure 90° corners.

3 Prepare wallcovering as on page 9. Apply wallcovering to surface of door, smoothing it in place with a damp sponge.

4 Trim the wallcovering about ⅛" (3 mm) from edges of door. This helps prevent the wallcovering from peeling back or fraying.

5 Apply wallcovering border to door, if desired; prepare border as on page 9, and miter corners, if necessary, as on page 13. Apply wallcovering cutouts to door, if desired, as on page 21. Complete screen as on page 67, steps 10 to 12.

HOW TO SHORTEN A HOLLOW-CORE DOOR

MATERIALS

- Circular saw.
- Utility knife; straightedge.
- Chisel; clamps.
- Wood glue.

1 Mark cutting line, using a straightedge. Cut through door veneer, using sharp utility knife, to prevent wood from splintering when the door is sawed.

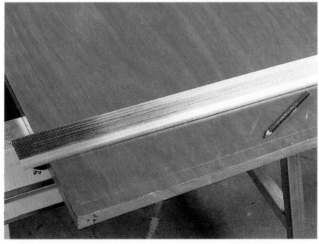

2 Lay the door on sawhorses; clamp a straightedge to the door as a cutting guide.

3 Saw off bottom of door, cutting on the marked line. If hollow core of door is exposed, continue as in steps 4 and 5, below.

4 Remove veneer from both sides of removed wood frame, using chisel.

5 Apply wood glue to both sides of frame. Insert frame into opening, and clamp in place; remove excess glue. Allow to dry overnight.

TUFTED
OTTOMANS

An ottoman can be a decorative accent in a room as well as provide extra seating. This circular ottoman is easily constructed using a plywood base and turned furniture legs with mounting plates. Tufting adds a distinctive look to the ottoman. The ottoman can be constructed without a skirt for a tailored look, or it may be constructed with a gathered skirt for a more feminine look.

The plywood base can easily be cut to size, using a jigsaw. Some lumber yards stock furniture-grade plywood circles, or will cut plywood to your specifications. Unfinished furniture legs with mounting plates are available in several styles and heights. Paint or stain the legs as desired before securing them to the ottoman base.

Most upholstery supply stores and fabric stores that sell upholstery foam will cut it to your specifications. For the tufting, use upholstery buttons custom-covered at an upholstery supply store; dressmaker's covered buttons are not strong enough.

An ottoman that has a 24" (61 cm) diameter can have a finished height of 13" to 20" (33 to 51 cm). Add 4" (10 cm) to the height of the legs to determine the finished height of the ottoman.

The ottoman base can be covered with 1¼ yd. (1.15 m) of fabric. Allow an additional ¾ yd. (0.7 m) of fabric for cutting the welting strips; it is not necessary for the strips to be cut on the true bias. The skirt is self-lined for drape and body. The skirt yardage required varies with the height of the legs.

***Ottoman** (opposite) has 14¼" (36.1 cm) legs that are hidden by a gathered skirt.*

***Ottoman** (above) is made without a skirt to expose the sleek, contemporary 9¼" (23.6 cm) wooden legs.*

MATERIALS

- Decorator fabric.
- Cambric or muslin, for dust cover on bottom of ottoman.
- 24" (61 cm) plywood circle, ¾" (2 cm) thick.
- 25" (63.5 cm) circle of firm 3" (7.5 cm) polyurethane foam.
- Aerosol foam adhesive.
- Seven upholstery buttons, size 22.
- Upholstery needle, 12" to 15" (30.5 to 38 cm) long; button twine.
- 2¼ yd. (2.1 m) cording, ⁵⁄₃₂" (3.8 mm) in diameter, for welting.
- Heavy-duty stapler (electric stapler is recommended) and ½" (1.3 cm) staples.
- 1 yd. (0.95 m) polyester upholstery batting, 57" (144.5 cm) wide.
- Four furniture legs with glides, in desired height; mounting plates for vertical leg mount.
- Drill and ½" drill bit.
- 2¼ yd. (2.1 m) cardboard stripping, for skirted ottoman.

CUTTING DIRECTIONS

Cut one 45" (115 cm) square from decorator fabric for covering the ottoman base. For the welting, cut bias fabric strips, 1⅝" (4 cm) wide, with the combined length of the strips equal to about 2¼ yd. (2.1 m). Cut the cambric or muslin for the dust cover on the bottom of the ottoman 1" (2.5 cm) larger than the plywood base.

For an ottoman with a gathered skirt, determine the finished skirt length by measuring the height of the leg with the mounting plate and adding ¾" (2 cm). The cut width of the skirt fabric is twice this measurement plus 1" (2.5 cm) for the seam allowances. The cut length of the skirt fabric measures about 4¼ yd. (3.9 m) for double fullness or about 5¼ yd. (4.8 m) for two and one-half times fullness; piece the strips as necessary for the required length.

HOW TO MAKE A TUFTED OTTOMAN

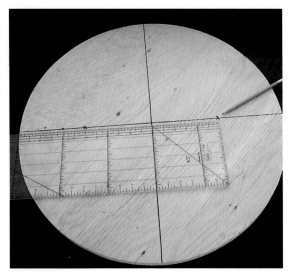

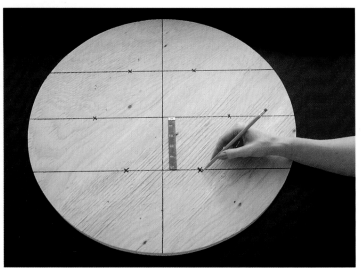

1 Draw two perpendicular lines dividing plywood into fourths. Mark points on horizontal line, 6" (15 cm) from center, on each side.

2 Draw line parallel to and 5⅛" (12.8 cm) above the line with the marked points. Draw another line parallel to and 5⅛" (12.8 cm) below the line with the marked points. Mark points on new lines, 3" (7.5 cm) from vertical line, on each side.

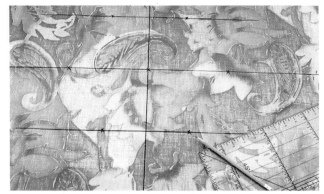

3 Repeat steps 1 and 2, using a pencil to mark lines and points on wrong side of fabric square; mark points 7¼" (18.7 cm) from center as in step 1, and position lines 5⅞" (14.7 cm) above and below previously marked line as in step 2. Mark points on each of these lines 3⅝" (9.3 cm) from vertical line. These marked points are a guide for tufting.

4 Drill ½" (1.3 cm) holes at center and at marked points on plywood. Apply aerosol foam adhesive to one side of plywood and to one side of foam; center plywood over foam, and press to secure.

5 Insert upholstery needle through hole in plywood; take care to insert needle straight down through foam. Mark point for tufting where needle exits foam. Repeat for the remaining holes.

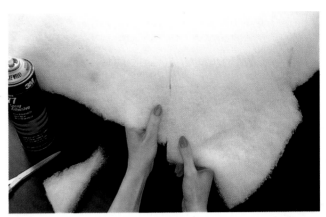

6 Center batting over foam. Cut hole, about 1" (2.5 cm) in diameter, through batting at locations corresponding to marked points on foam.

7 Secure batting to foam, using aerosol foam adhesive; align holes in batting with the marked points on foam. Wrap the batting around sides, securing with foam adhesive; cut and remove wedges as necessary for smooth fit. Trim the batting even with lower edge of plywood.

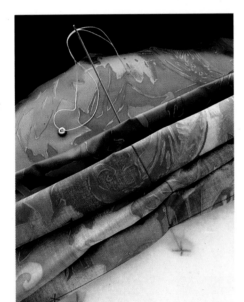

8 Position the fabric, right side up, over the foam, aligning markings for tufting. Thread button onto 32" (81.5 cm) length of button twine. Fold twine in half; thread both ends into the upholstery needle, leaving 5" (12.5 cm) tails. With center point of fabric and foam aligned, push needle through the fabric, foam, and hole in plywood.

9 Pull twine firmly, indenting foam. Pull twine to the side, stapling securely three or four times over twine so it will not slip.

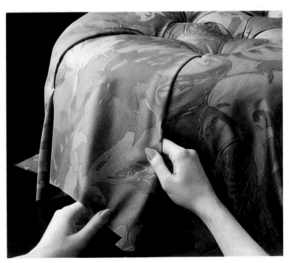

10 Repeat steps 8 and 9 to tuft a diamond-shaped area as shown; smooth the fabric in place before inserting needle, and use marked points as a guide for the needle placement. Straighten tucks formed between buttons with blunt end of the needle. Complete remaining diamond-shaped tuft.

11 Smooth and pin fabric around sides of base; remove as much excess fullness as possible by folding a tuck at each outer button. Adjust tucks for even spacing.

(Continued)

12 Staple fabric to the underside of the plywood, about ¾" (2 cm) from edge, wrapping fabric firmly around sides; any excess fullness may be distributed by making smaller tucks between the larger tucks. It may be necessary to periodically remove staples and reposition fabric. Trim excess fabric close to staples.

13 Make welting as on page 90, step 1. Staple welting around edge of ottoman base at ¾" (2 cm) intervals, starting 2" (5 cm) from end of the welting; align stitching line of welting to edge of base.

14 Stop stapling 3" (7.5 cm) from first staple. Cut off the end of the welting so it overlaps the other end by 1" (2.5 cm).

15 Remove 1" (2.5 cm) of stitching from one end of welting. Trim ends of cording so they just meet.

16 Fold under ½" (1.3 cm) of the fabric on the overlapping end of welting; lap it around the other end. Finish stapling the welting to the ottoman base.

17 Staple cambric or muslin to the bottom of ottoman at 1" (2.5 cm) intervals, turning under about 1" (2.5 cm) on raw edges.

18 Position mounting plates for legs on plywood, spacing them evenly; position the mounting plates about 1" (2.5 cm) from the edge of plywood. Predrill holes for screws; secure mounting plates. Attach legs.

1 Follow steps 1 to 12 on pages 72 to 74; in step 7, trim batting even with lower edge of the foam. Continue as in steps 17 and 18, opposite; do not attach legs. Make the welting as on page 90, step 1. Pin-mark 1½" (3.8 cm) from one end. Staple-baste welting around edge of ottoman base as shown; stretch taut, and pin-mark where welting meets first pin. Trim the welting 1½" (3.8 cm) from pin mark, and remove welting from base.

2 Stitch short ends of ottoman skirt together in ½" (1.3 cm) seam, forming continuous strip; press seam open. Fold skirt in half, wrong sides together, matching raw edges; press.

3 Zigzag over a cord at upper edge of skirt, within seam allowance, just inside the seamline. For more control when adjusting the gathers, zigzag over second cord, ¼" (6 mm) from the first.

4 Divide welting strip and skirt into fourths; pin-mark. Pin welting to right side of skirt, matching pin marks and positioning pin marks near ends of welting at ends of gathering cords. Gather skirt to fit welting strip. Stitch along previous stitching, starting and stopping 1" (2.5 cm) from pin marks.

5 Position the ottoman base upside down. Place skirt around ottoman base, right sides together. Position the raw edges of the skirt and welting a scant ¼" (6 mm) below edge of the plywood as shown; welting seamline aligns with other edge of plywood.

7 Finish the ends of welting as in steps 14 to 16, opposite. Gather remaining skirt to fit; secure with cardboard stripping and staples. Trim excess cardboard stripping so ends butt together. Attach legs. Stand ottoman on legs; smooth skirt into place.

6 Position cardboard stripping over the seam allowance, aligning the upper edges of skirt and cardboard stripping; staple through all layers into the edge of plywood at 1" (2.5 cm) intervals.

WALLCOVERING ON FURNITURE

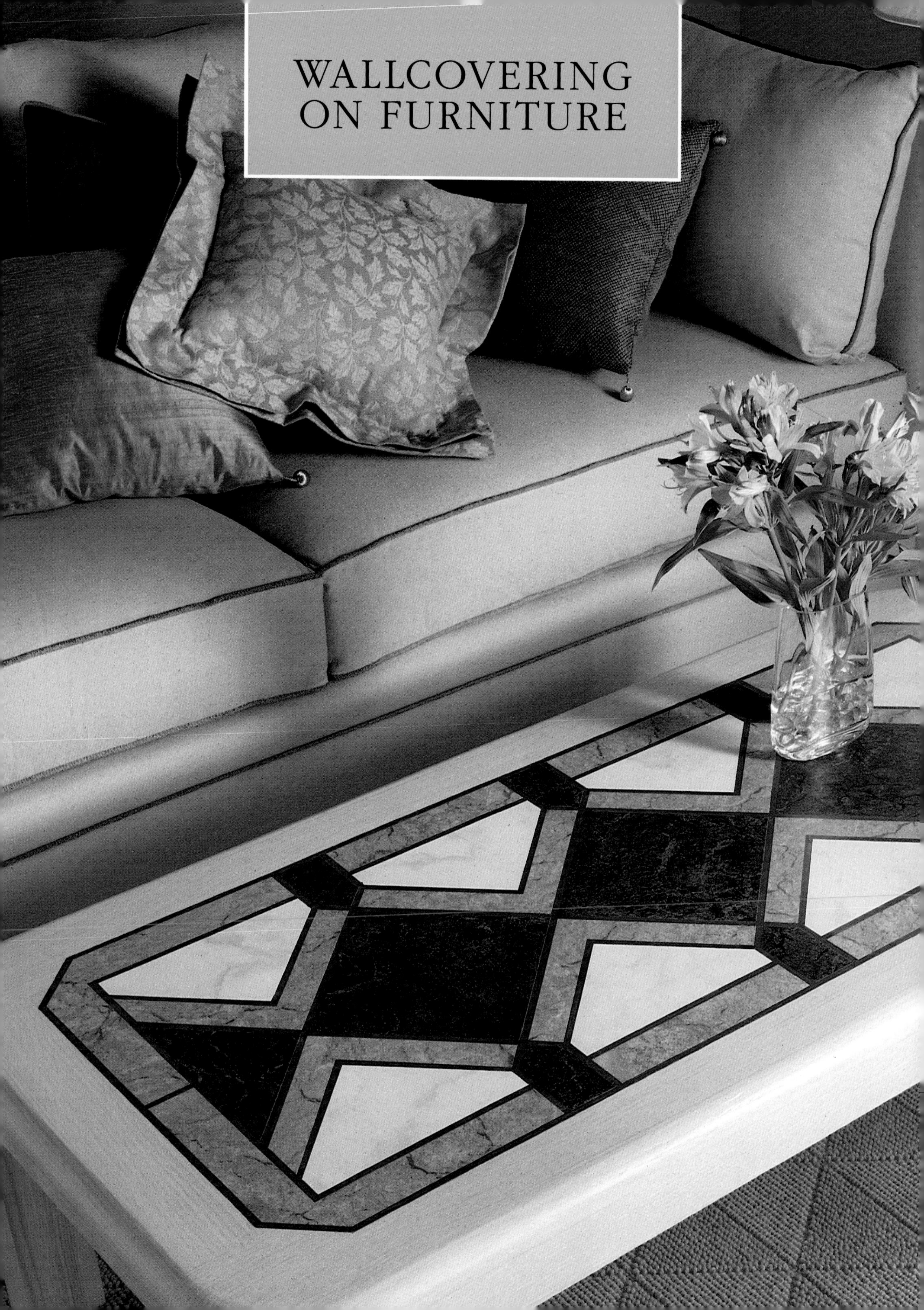

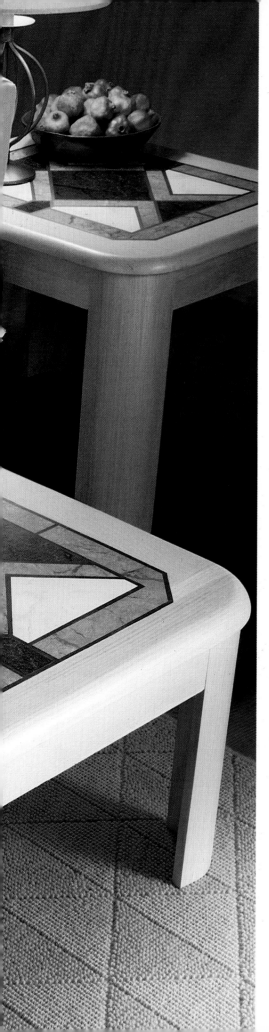

Embellish tables and the flat surfaces of other furniture, such as trunks, dressers, and cabinets, with wallcovering to create distinctive furniture and accent pieces. For a quick embellishment, apply borders or cutouts. For a more intricate look, create your own custom design to imitate the look of tile or inlay. For this look, the wallcovering pieces are separated by narrow sections painted to simulate grout or spacers.

Tile or inlay designs can be as simple as cutting one wallcovering into squares, or use several wallcoverings and more intricate pieces to create complex designs. Inlay designs are especially attractive when made from wallcoverings that imitate marble or stone. The paint chosen to imitate grout lines or spacers must be compatible with the surface being painted.

Wallcovering can be applied to most furniture surfaces, including metal, varnished, painted, and laminate. Apply the wallcovering using a border adhesive; this adhesive is suitable for all surfaces and ensures a strong bond.

To protect the wallcovering and to seal the edges, apply several coats of a clear finish, such as water-based polyurethane or acrylic finish, to the embellished surface. This finish can be applied over most surfaces and is easy to work with. For durability, select a finish that is recommended for surfaces that receive heavy use.

Wallcovering can be used to add design interest to ordinary furniture. Opposite, the inlay designs on the coffee table and end table are made by cutting three different wallcoverings into design shapes. The spacer lines are indicated by gold paint. Above, a fruit basket wallcovering cutout creates a focal point on a desk. Wallcovering border edging strips outline the drawers and the top of the desk.

HOW TO APPLY A WALLCOVERING BORDER & CUTOUTS TO FURNITURE

MATERIALS

- Wallcovering border and cutouts as desired.
- Ammonia, for cleaning furniture surface.
- Fine-grit sandpaper, for deglossing shiny surfaces.
- Border adhesive.
- Sponge applicator; sponge; seam roller.

- Mat knife and cutting surface, or small sharp scissors.
- Clear finish, such as water-based polyurethane or acrylic.
- Permanent markers or colored pencils, in colors to match the furniture surface or the edges of wallcovering, optional.

1 Clean furniture surface, using a solution of equal parts of ammonia and water, to remove any grease or soil. Degloss areas of shiny surfaces that will be covered with wallcovering, by lightly sanding with fine-grit sandpaper. This improves adhesion for the adhesive and clear finish.

2 Cut design motifs from wallcovering. White cut edges of wallcovering may be colored, using a permanent marker or colored pencil that matches furniture surface or wallcovering.

3 Arrange designs on surface as desired; lightly mark the position, using a pencil.

4 Apply an even coat of border adhesive to the back side of the wallcovering, using a sponge applicator. Press the wallcovering on furniture surface; smooth out any air bubbles, using damp sponge. Cut any mitered borders as on page 13; immediately roll edges and seams of wallcovering firmly with a seam roller. Allow to dry thoroughly.

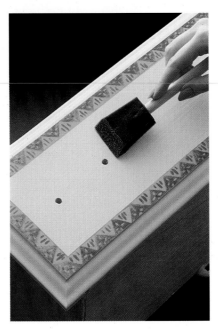

5 Apply clear finish to the embellished surface, using a sponge applicator and following the manufacturer's directions; allow to dry. Repeat to apply three or more coats.

HOW TO APPLY WALLCOVERING TO FURNITURE
IN A TILED OR INLAID DESIGN

MATERIALS

- Wallcovering.
- Ammonia, for cleaning furniture surfaces.
- Fine-grit sandpaper, for deglossing shiny surfaces.
- Sheet of paper; transfer paper.
- Paint, for simulated grout or spacer lines.
- ¼" (6 mm) tape, for marking simulated grout or spacer lines.
- Painter's masking tape.

- Border adhesive.
- Sponge applicator; sponge; seam roller.
- Mat knife or rotary cutter and cutting surface.
- Clear finish, such as water-based polyurethane or acrylic.
- Permanent markers or colored pencils, in colors to match the furniture surface or the edges of wallcovering, optional.

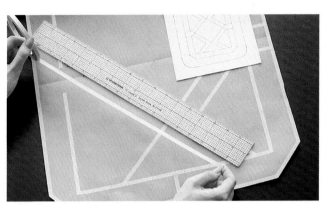

1 Measure the dimensions of furniture, and plan design on graph paper. Cut sheet of paper to design size, and mark points where design lines intersect. Use ¼" (6 mm) tape and straightedge to mark grout or spacer lines on paper. It may be helpful to fold the paper into equal sections before marking design.

2 Prepare furniture surface as in step 1, opposite. Tape off outer edge of the design on furniture with painter's masking tape. Transfer any complex designs using transfer paper; simple designs may be transferred using straightedge and pencil.

3 Label top side of each design piece. Cut paper pattern apart along edges of tape lines; discard ¼" (6 mm) tape strips. Tape pattern pieces to wallcovering, top side up; cut design pieces. The white cut edges of the wallcovering may be colored, using permanent marker or colored pencil that matches the furniture surface or wallcovering.

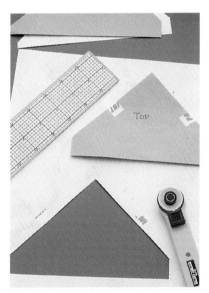

4 Paint over marked lines, applying paint wider than the ¼" (6 mm) needed for grout or spacers; wallcovering pieces will partially cover the paint, leaving ¼" (6 mm) between the pieces.

5 Position wallcovering designs on the furniture surface; lightly mark placement lines. Complete project as in steps 4 and 5, opposite; if wallcovering expands after the adhesive is applied, trim pieces to size, using a mat knife.

MORE IDEAS FOR
WALLCOVERING ON FURNITURE

Table and chairs are embellished with wallcovering cutouts. Plate motifs cut from a border embellish the table. A floral motif cut from a different wallcovering decorates each chair back.

Children's toy chest (above) is decorated with cars, trucks, and airplanes cut from a wallcovering border. Other wallcovering pieces are applied to the top and the lower edge of the chest.

Cabinet (left) has wallcovering applied to the inside of the door panels to create a trompe l'oeil effect.

Chest (below), painted with black paint, is embellished with Chinese-style motifs and border edging strips cut from wallcovering.

Room
Accessories

TAPESTRIES

Tapestry fabrics can be used to create decorative wall hangings, throws, or area rugs. The tapestry projects shown here are each made by surrounding a center panel with a mitered border.

The maximum size of the center panel is limited to the width of the fabric. Most tapestries are 54" (137 cm) wide. Additional width can be achieved by adding a border on all sides. Customized tapestry borders can be made by cutting strips from striped tapestry fabrics. Tapestry borders are also available on bolts at some fabric stores.

The tapestry wall hangings feature tabs along the upper edge so they may be displayed on decorative poles or rods. Tapestry wall hangings may be used instead of paintings or pictures to bring texture and color to rooms.

Throws can be square or rectangular in shape. For a generous square throw, use the full width of the fabric for the center panel. Rectangular throws are generally 6 ft. (1.85 m) long. Select a lining fabric for the back side of the throw that coordinates with the tapestry pattern, such as a lightweight damask or cotton sateen. For additional interest, apply fringe to the ends of the throw or around all four sides.

Tapestry rugs add a touch of drama to a room. These rugs are best suited to low-traffic areas. In general, the length of an area rug is about one and one-half times the width of the rug. For added detail, insert cotton fringe at the ends of the rug. If the rug will be placed on a smooth floor surface, such as linoleum or ceramic, use a nonslip pad under the rug.

Bordered tapestries *add visual interest to a room. Above, the southwestern-style wall hanging features decorative tabs and measures 24" × 25" (61 × 63.5 cm). Opposite, the throw has a narrow mitered border and is embellished with extra-long bullion fringe. Below, the tapestry rug features knotted cotton fringe at each end.*

HOW TO SEW A TAPESTRY WALL HANGING, RUG, OR THROW

MATERIALS

- Two coordinating tapestry fabrics or one tapestry fabric and one border tapestry, yardage depending on size of project.
- Backing fabric, such as mediumweight cotton, in color to match tapestry, for wall hanging or rug; lining fabric, for throw.
- Fringe and liquid fray preventer, for throw or rug, optional.
- Rod, 1" (2.5 cm) in diameter, for wall hanging.

CUTTING DIRECTIONS

Determine the desired length and width of the finished tapestry, taking into consideration the printed designs on the fabric. To determine the cut size of the center panel, subtract two times the desired finished width of the border from the finished length and width of the tapestry; then add 1" (2.5 cm), to allow for ½" (1.3 cm) seam allowances.

You will need four border strips, with the cut width equal to the desired finished width of the border plus 1" (2.5 cm). To determine the length of the border strips, add two times the cut width of the border plus 2" (5 cm) to the measurement of the cut side of the middle panel; cut two border strips based on the width of the middle panel and two based on the length of the panel.

For wall hangings, determine the desired finished width of the tabs; then determine the spacing and number of tabs desired. Cut one strip of tapestry fabric for each tab, cutting the strips ¾" (2 cm) wider and 1" (2.5 cm) longer than the desired finished size. Cut the same number of strips from the backing fabric, with the width of the strips ½" (1.3 cm) wider and 1" (2.5 cm) longer than the desired finished size.

Cut the lining as in step 7, opposite, after the border has been applied.

1 Mark the middle panel at center of each side, on wrong side of fabric; mark center of each border strip on wrong side.

2 Mark the middle panel at all corners, ½" (1.3 cm) from each raw edge, on wrong side of fabric.

4 Fold the middle panel diagonally at the corners, matching border seams and raw edges of border strips. Place straightedge along fold; draw stitching line for mitered seam on border, using chalk. Stitching line should be at 45° angle to raw edges.

3 Pin one border strip to one side of middle panel, right sides together, matching the raw edges and centers. Stitch border strip to middle panel in ½" (1.3 cm) seam, starting and ending at corner markings. Repeat for remaining border strips.

5 Pin mitered seam, and stitch, beginning at raw edge and ending at the previous seamline. Trim the seam allowances on the mitered corners to ½" (1.3 cm).

6 Trim middle panel diagonally across corners of border seam, and trim off outer points of mitered border; clip the seam allowances of border strips to the corner stitching. Apply liquid fray preventer to trimmed and clipped edges. Press all seams open. Apply fringe to the rug or throw, if desired (below). Apply tabs to wall hanging (below).

7 Cut the lining ¼" to ½" (6 mm to 1.3 cm) shorter than the length and width of bordered top; this prevents the lining from showing on the right side at the edges. Pin the lining to the bordered top, right sides together, matching raw edges.

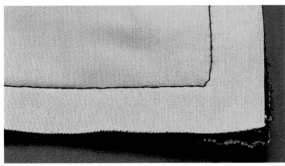

8 Stitch ½" (1.3 cm) seam on all sides, lining side up, taking one diagonal stitch across the corners; leave opening on one side for turning.

9 Trim seam allowances diagonally across the corners; apply liquid fray preventer. Press the lining seam allowance toward lining. Turn right side out; press. Hand-stitch the opening closed.

HOW TO APPLY FRINGE & TABS TO TAPESTRIES

1 Tabs. Place one tapestry tab strip and one backing strip right sides together, matching raw edges. Stitch ¼" (6 mm) seam on long edges. Repeat for remaining tabs. Turn tabs right side out, and press.

Fringe. Machine-baste fringe to front side of rug or throw, with heading of fringe within seam allowance; curve heading around any corners, and fold back about ½" (1.3 cm) at ends of heading. Apply liquid fray preventer to cut ends.

2 Fold tabs in half, and pin to front side of wall hanging at the upper edge, matching the raw edges. Position the tabs 1" (2.5 cm) from the ends; space the remaining tabs evenly between the end tabs. Machine-baste tabs in place.

TAILORED TABLE COVERS

Tailored table covers can be made to fit any round, square, or rectangular table, from accent tables to dining tables. Inverted pleats, placed evenly around the skirt, add style and fullness. Welting complements the tailored style and adds definition around the edges of the tabletop. Use these tailored table covers to conceal less-than-perfect tables or to add color and texture to a room. Because the table cover is floor-length, the area under the table can also double as storage space.

Allow at least 12" (30.5 cm) of fabric for each inverted pleat. If the table will be used for dining, allow 20" (51 cm) for each pleat to allow room for sliding chairs under the table. Plan for a pleat at each corner of square or rectangular tables. More fullness can be created by centering additional pleats on the sides, between the corner pleats, if desired. For round tables, space the pleats about 20" to 30" (51 to 76 cm) apart, depending on the size of the table.

The table skirt can be made from one continuous length of fabric, if the fabric is cut so the lengthwise grain is used horizontally around the table. Or, for fabric with a one-way design, shorter panels can be stitched together at the sides until the desired length is achieved. For seamed panels, plan the seam placement so the seams will be concealed within a pleat whenever possible. If it is necessary to piece the fabric for the top, avoid a center seam by using a full fabric width as a center panel, stitching it to narrow side panels to achieve the necessary width.

MATERIALS

- Decorator fabric.
- ⁵⁄₃₂" (3.8 mm) cording, for welting.
- Flat trim, such as braid or grosgrain ribbon.

CUTTING DIRECTIONS

For a square or rectangular table, cut one top piece from fabric equal to the dimensions of the tabletop plus 1" (2.5 cm) for ½" (1.3 cm) seam allowances. For a table with rounded corners, make a pattern for the tabletop, adding ½" (1.3 cm) seam allowances. For a round tabletop, follow steps 1 and 2 on page 91 to cut the top piece.

Determine the length of the table skirt by measuring from the upper edge of the table to ¼" (6 mm) above the floor; add 1" (2.5 cm) for ½" (1.3 cm) seam allowances. Determine the width of the skirt by measuring the circumference of the table; add 12" to 20" (30.5 to 51 cm) for each pleat plus 1" (2.5 cm) for each seam. Cut the skirt, using these measurements.

For the welting, cut bias fabric strips, 1⅝" (4 cm) wide; piece the strips as necessary for a length equal to the circumference of the table plus 2" (5 cm) for overlap.

Tailored table covers *can be used on large or small tables. The rectangular cover above is used on a dining table and features braid trim along the lower edge. The table cover opposite is made for a round table and has grosgrain ribbon trim.*

HOW TO MAKE A SQUARE OR RECTANGULAR
TAILORED TABLE COVER

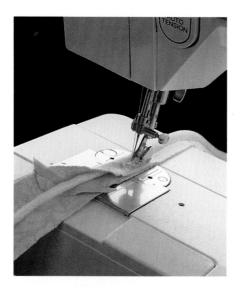

1 Seam welting strips together. Fold strip around cording, wrong sides together, matching the raw edges. Using a zipper foot, machine-baste close to cording.

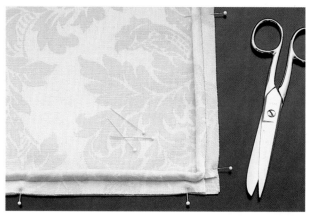

2 Pin welting to right side of top piece, with raw edges aligned; clip welting at corners. Stitch welting to table top piece, starting 2" (5 cm) from end of welting; stitch over previous stitches.

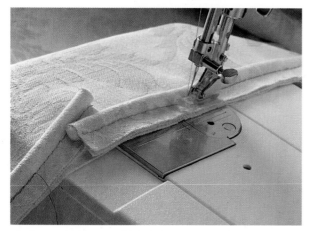

3 Stop stitching 2" (5 cm) from point where cording ends will meet. Leaving needle in fabric, cut off one end of cording so it overlaps other end by 1" (2.5 cm).

4 Remove 1" (2.5 cm) of the stitching from one end of welting. Trim cording ends so they just meet. Fold under ½" (1.3 cm) of overlapping fabric; lap around other end. Finish stitching.

5 Join the skirt panels in ½" (1.3 cm) seams; finish seams. Pin braid trim to lower edge of skirt, with the wrong sides together, so edge of trim overlaps the skirt by ½" (1.3 cm). Cut off end of trim so it overlaps other end by 1" (2.5 cm). Turn under ½" (1.3 cm) on one short end of trim; pin.

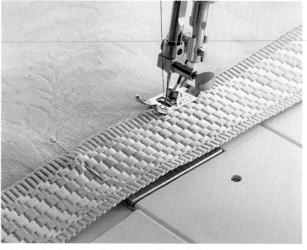

6 Stitch close to the inner edge of the trim.

7 Fold trim to right side; press. Stitch close to inner edge of trim. Edgestitch close to the outer edge of trim, if desired. Slipstitch short ends together.

8 Pin-mark the placement of the pleats on top piece. Measure and pin-mark the center of each pleat on upper edge of the skirt. Clip-mark skirt on both sides of pin marks, a distance equal to one-half the measurement allowed for each of the pleats.

9 Fold the clip marks to pin marks to make inverted pleats; press. Baste the pleats in place ⅜" (1 cm) from raw edge of fabric.

10 Pin skirt to top piece, with right sides together and the raw edges even; match center of pleats to the pin marks on the top piece. Clip center of each corner pleat to, but not through, stitching. Stitch skirt to top just inside previous stitching.

HOW TO MAKE A ROUND TAILORED TABLE COVER

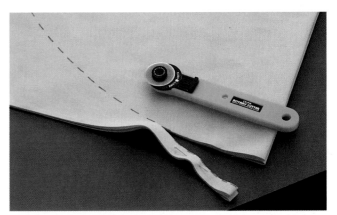

1 Measure diameter of the table; add 1" (2.5 cm) for seam allowances. Cut a square of fabric at least this size; piece fabric widths together, if necessary, and press seams open. Fold the fabric square in half lengthwise, then crosswise.

2 Divide measurement for diameter of fabric circle by two, to determine radius. Mark an arc on fabric, using a straightedge and pencil, measuring from folded center of fabric, a distance equal to radius. Cut on the marked line through all layers. Complete as in steps 1 to 10, opposite, ignoring any references to corners; clip welting and ease to skirt as necessary for smooth fit.

SLIPCOVERS

Two-piece slipcovers can be used on simple kitchen or dining-room chairs to update a look or to help soften the room with fabric. Slipcovers can also be used to cover up worn or unmatched chairs. Slipcover styles can range from country to formal, depending on the fabric choice and detailing of the chair. Both the back and the seat slipcovers are lined for durability and body. Welting, applied around the seat slipcover and along the lower edge of the back slipcover, adds a finishing touch.

The back slipcover and the skirt on the chair seat can be long or short. When determining the desired back length and skirt length of the slipcovers, take into account the style and detailing of the chair. For a nice drape and an attractive appearance, make the skirt at least 5" to 6" (12.5 to 15 cm) long and end the skirt slightly above or below any cross pieces of the chair. Chairs with seats that slope toward the back will have skirts that also slope toward the back, making the fabric hang slightly off-grain at the side back of the chair. For this reason, avoid long skirt styles on chairs that have sloping seats. It may also be desirable to avoid fabrics with obvious stripes, plaids, or one-way designs on chairs of this style.

The seat slipcover can be made with either pleats or clustered gathers at the front corners. Select chairs with an open back at the edge of the seat to allow decorative ties to be secured to the back posts. Concealed twill-tape ties secure the cover to the front legs of the chair.

For back slipcovers that are long, the back of the chair must be straight from the seat to the upper edge of the back or taper slightly inward; if the upper edge of the chair back is wider than the lower edge, it will not be possible to slip the cover on. However, short slipcovers, covering one-third to one-half of the back, may be suitable for this style chair. You may want to test-fit a muslin pattern before purchasing the decorator fabric.

MATERIALS

- Muslin, for patterns.
- Decorator fabric.
- Lining fabric.
- 1" (2.5 cm) twill tape.
- 5⁄32" (3.8 mm) cording, for optional welting.

Slipcovers can be designed to offer either a casual or a formal look. The short, casual slipcovers opposite have skirts with clustered gathers at the front corners. At right, the tailored slipcover has a full-length back and skirt. The skirt features inverted pleats at the front corners.

CUTTING DIRECTIONS

Make the seat and back patterns as on pages 94 and 95. Cut one seat each from outer fabric and lining; transfer the markings. For a gathered skirt, cut the fabric as on page 95, steps 1 and 2. For a skirt with corner pleats, cut the fabric as on page 97, step 1. Cut eight fabric strips 1½" (3.8 cm) wide and 10" to 16" (25.5 to 40.5 cm) long for the back ties on the seat cover. Cut four 12" (30.5 cm) lengths of twill tape for the concealed front ties. Using the pattern for a straight or shaped slipcover back (pages 94 and 95), cut one front and one back from both the outer fabric and lining; transfer the markings.

If welting is desired, cut 1⅝" (4 cm) bias strips. The combined length of the strips is equal to the circumference of the seat cover and the lower edge of the back cover; allow extra for seams and overlaps.

HOW TO MAKE A CHAIR SEAT SLIPCOVER PATTERN

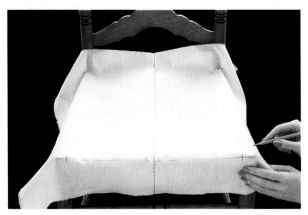

1 Measure the chair seat; cut muslin about 6" (15 cm) larger than measurements. Mark the center line on lengthwise grain. Center muslin on seat; pin or tape in place. Using pencil, mark outer rim of seat front, and sides to back posts, rounding square corners slightly. Mark placement for front ties.

2 Mark back edge of chair seat on muslin; clip the fabric as necessary for snug fit if seat is shaped around back posts. On muslin, mark the placement of skirt back between the chair posts.

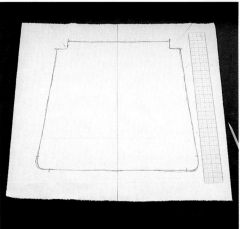

3 Remove muslin from the chair. Redraw seamlines as necessary, using a straightedge; redraw curved lines, drawing smooth curves. Reposition muslin on chair; adjust as necessary.

4 Add ½" (1.3 cm) seam allowances. Cut pattern on marked lines.

HOW TO MAKE A CHAIR BACK SLIPCOVER PATTERN

1 Straight upper edge. Measure chair back; cut two pieces of muslin about 6" (15 cm) wider and 2" (5 cm) longer than measurements. Mark a line, 1" (2.5 cm) from raw edge, for upper edge of chair back; pin pieces together on the marked line. Center the muslin on the chair with the marked line at upper edge.

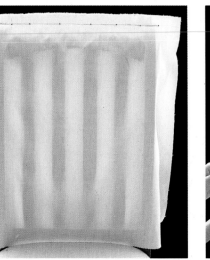

2 Pin muslin at sides of chair, allowing ample ease. Mark desired finished length. Pull gently on cover to make sure it slides off easily; adjust width or length of cover, if necessary.

3 Mark seamlines, following pin placement. Label patterns for front and back.

4 Remove muslin from the chair. Redraw seamlines as necessary, using straightedge. Repin muslin, and position on chair; adjust as necessary. Front and back of pattern may be different sizes.

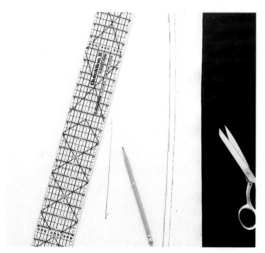

5 Mark ½" (1.3 cm) seam allowances; mark grainline. Cut pattern on marked lines.

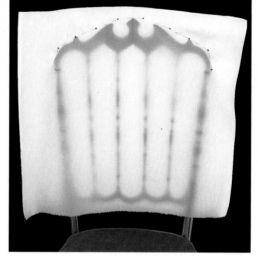

Shaped upper edge. Measure chair back; cut two pieces of muslin about 6" (15 cm) larger than measurements. Pin pieces together at the upper edge, and center over chair back; adjust pins to follow contours of the chair, simplifying design as necessary. Continue as for chair back with straight upper edge, steps 2 to 4, opposite; in step 4, smooth any curved lines. Complete pattern as in step 5.

HOW TO SEW A CHAIR SEAT SLIPCOVER WITH GATHERED CORNERS

1 Measure pattern seamline around the front and sides of seat between markings at the back posts; add 12" (30.5 cm) for the corner gathers plus 1" (2.5 cm) for seam allowances. Cut the fabric strip for front skirt to this length, piecing fabric, if necessary; width of strip is equal to twice the desired finished skirt length plus 1" (2.5 cm) for seam allowances.

2 Measure pattern seamline between markings for back skirt. Cut fabric strip for back skirt to this length plus 1" (2.5 cm); width of strip is equal to twice the desired finished skirt length plus 1" (2.5 cm) for seam allowances.

(Continued)

3 Staystitch any inner corners and curves on chair seat top and lining. Clip to, but not through, stitching as necessary.

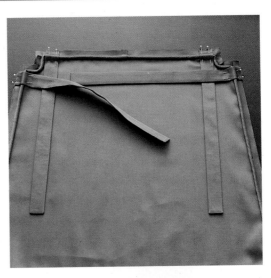

4 Make welting, if desired, and apply to seat top as on page 90, steps 1 to 4. Stitch strips for decorative ties as on page 111, step 3. Pin ties to the right side of seat top at back corners as desired, aligning raw edges.

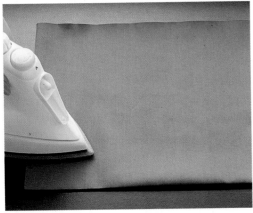

5 Fold the skirt front in half lengthwise, right sides together; stitch ½" (1.3 cm) seams on short ends. Turn right side out; press. Repeat for skirt back.

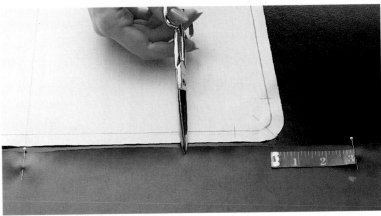

6 Pin-mark center of skirt at raw edges. Measure edge of seat pattern on seamline, from center front to corner; add 3" (7.5 cm). Measure this distance out from center of skirt, and pin-mark for corners. Clip-mark skirt 6" (15 cm) from both sides of corner pin marks.

7 Stitch two rows of gathering threads along upper edge of skirt front between clip marks, ¼" (6 mm) and ½" (1.3 cm) from raw edges.

8 Pin skirt front to the seat top, right sides together, matching the raw edges and markings for center front and corners. Pull gathering threads to fit. Machine-baste skirt to seat top, using zipper foot.

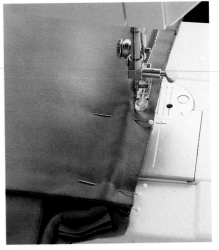

9 Pin skirt back to the seat top, right sides together, matching the raw edges; stitch, using zipper foot.

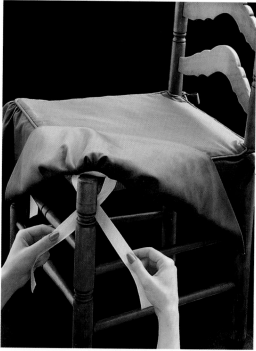

10 Pin or baste twill-tape ties to wrong side of skirt at front-corner tie markings.

11 Pin skirt and ties to the seat to prevent catching them in seam allowance. Pin lining to the seat, with right sides together and raw edges even. Stitch, leaving a 6" (15 cm) center opening on back of seat. Trim seam allowances; clip curves and corners.

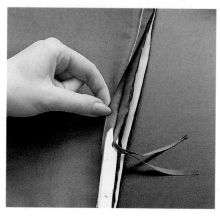

12 Turn the seat cover right side out; press. Slipstitch opening closed. Position seat cover on chair; secure the back ties in a bow or a square knot. Lift skirt, and secure front ties; trim excess length.

HOW TO SEW A CHAIR SEAT SLIPCOVER WITH CORNER PLEATS

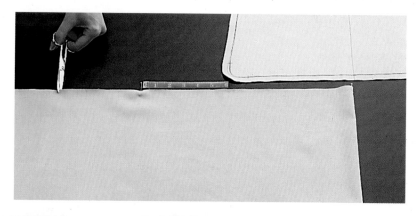

1 Follow steps 1 to 5 on pages 95 and 96; in step 1, add 24" (61 cm) instead of 12" (30.5 cm). Pin-mark the center of the skirt at raw edges. Measure outer edge of seat pattern on seamline, from center front to corner, and add 6" (15 cm); measure this distance from center of skirt front, and pin-mark for corners. Clip-mark the fabric 6" (15 cm) from both sides of the corner pin marks.

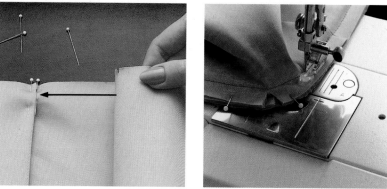

2 Fold 3" (7.5 cm) inverted pleats at front corners, matching the clip marks to the corner pin marks; press. Machine-baste the pleats in place.

3 Pin the skirt front to the seat top, right sides together, matching raw edges and markings for center front and corners; clip skirt at the corners as necessary. Machine-baste skirt to seat top. Complete skirt as in steps 9 to 12, opposite.

1 Straight upper edge. Place the front and the back outer fabric pieces right sides together, matching the raw edges. Stitch ½" (1.3 cm) seam around sides and upper edge. Press seam open.

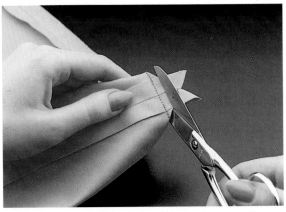

2 To accommodate depth of chair, open out the corners, aligning seam allowances; stitch across corners, a distance equal to the depth of the chair. Trim seam.

3 Attach welting, if desired, to lower edge of outer cover as on page 90, steps 1 to 4. Stitch lining as for outer cover, leaving a 6" (15 cm) center opening on one side. Press seam allowances open.

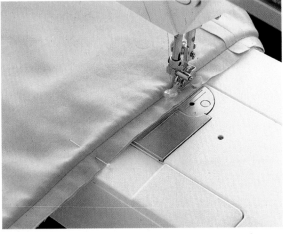

4 Place outer fabric and lining right sides together, matching lower edge; stitch ½" (1.3 cm) seam.

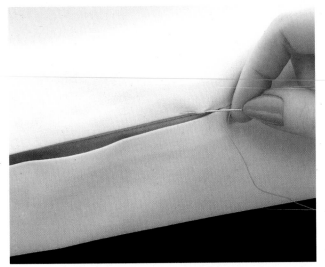

5 Turn slipcover, lining side out, through the opening in the lining; press the lower edge. Slipstitch opening closed. Turn slipcover right side out; place over back of chair.

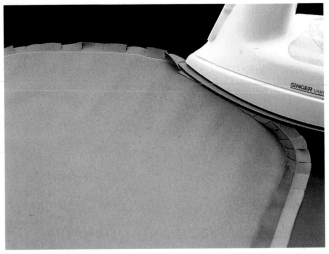

Shaped upper edge. Place the front and back outer fabric pieces right sides together, matching raw edges. Stitch ½" (1.3 cm) seam around sides and upper edge; press open. Trim seam; clip any curves. Complete as in steps 3 to 5.

MORE IDEAS FOR SLIPCOVERS

Coordinating fabrics *are used to cover a pair of unmatched porch chairs (right). One slipcover has a skirt gathered to double fullness. The other slipcover features a skirt with corner pleats. It has additional welting around the sides and upper edge of the chair back. The ties on both chair covers, made 4" (10 cm) wide, create the large bows.*

Buttons *(below) accent the pleats of the chair skirt and add detail to the lower edge of the back slipcover.*

Grosgrain ribbon *provides contrast along the lower edges of this chair back and skirt. Apply the grosgrain ribbon by edgestitching along both sides.*

BUTTON-TUFTED CUSHIONS

Add seating comfort to wooden chairs and benches with simple knife-edge, button-tufted cushions. The lightly padded inner cushion is created by covering a piece of foam with a layer of polyester upholstery batting. The button tufting prevents the cushion from shifting inside the cover and also adds detailing. Place one button on the top and one on the bottom of the cushion, and pull them tight with strands of thread to create an indentation. Welting can be inserted into the seam for additional interest.

You may want to make the covered buttons and welting from a fabric that contrasts with that of the seat cushion. Checked and striped fabrics can create interesting effects when used for welting.

Secure the seat cushion to the chairs or benches with ties, if necessary. Place a set of ties near each back corner of the cushion for securing it to the back posts of the chair or bench.

HOW TO MAKE A BUTTON-TUFTED CUSHION

MATERIALS

- Decorator fabric.
- Contrasting decorator fabric, for buttons and welting, optional.
- Polyurethane foam, 1" (2.5 cm) thick.
- Polyester upholstery batting; polyester fiberfill, optional.
- Cording, 5/32" (3.8 mm) in diameter, for welting, optional.
- Upholstery buttons or flat dressmaker buttons with strong shank; two for each button placement.
- Buttonhole twist or carpet thread; long needle with large eye.

CUTTING DIRECTIONS

Make the pattern and cut the fabric, foam, and batting following steps 1 to 3, below. For the optional welting, cut 1⅝" (4 cm) bias fabric strips; piece the strips as necessary to make a length that is equal to the circumference of the cushion plus at least 1" (2.5 cm) overlap at the ends. For each tie, cut two 1½" (3.8 cm) fabric strips 10" to 16" (25.5 to 40.5 cm) long.

1 Make a paper pattern of seat to be covered by cushion, rounding any sharp corners; simplify shape as necessary. Cut pattern; check the fit. Mark pattern for placement of ties, if desired.

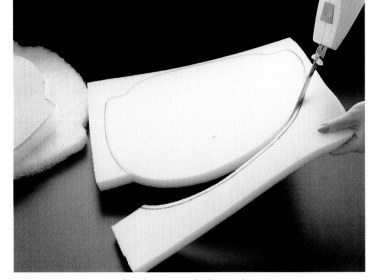

2 Cut two pieces of polyester upholstery batting, using pattern. Position pattern on foam; trace, using marking pen. Cut foam ¼" (6 mm) inside marked line, using electric or serrated knife.

3 Position the pattern on wrong side of decorator fabric. Mark cutting line 1" (2.5 cm) from edge of pattern; this allows ½" (1.3 cm) for the seam allowances and ½" (1.3 cm) for the thickness of the foam and batting. Cut the cushion top on marked line. Cut cushion bottom, using cushion top as pattern.

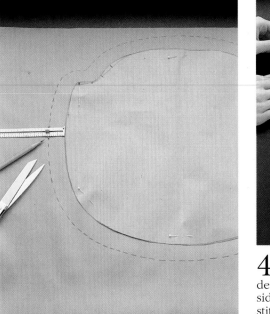

4 Make welting, if desired, and apply to cushion top as on page 90, steps 1 to 4. Make ties, if desired, as on page 111, step 3. Pin ties to the right side of seat top at markings, with raw edges even; stitch in place.

5 Position cushion top and bottom with right sides together and raw edges even. Stitch ½" (1.3 cm) seam; leave center opening along back edge for inserting cushion. Trim the seam allowances and clip curves. If welting is not used, press seam open. Turn right side out; lightly press.

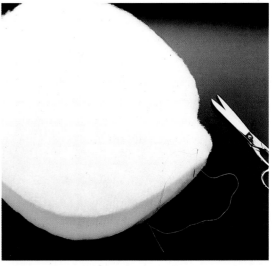

6 Place foam between layers of batting; hand-baste edges of batting together, encasing foam.

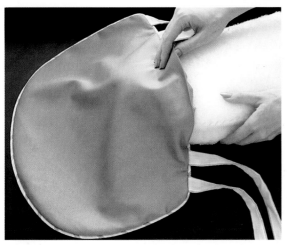

7 Fold the foam in half; insert into fabric cover. Flatten foam, smoothing the fabric over batting. Insert polyester fiberfill into corners, if necessary. Slipstitch opening closed.

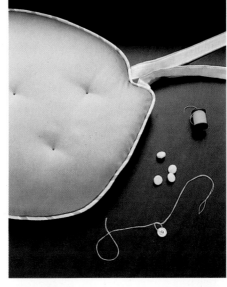

8 Pin-mark button placement on both sides of cushion as desired. Cut two or three 18" (45 cm) strands of buttonhole twist or carpet thread; insert all strands through button shank, and secure at middle of thread length with a double knot.

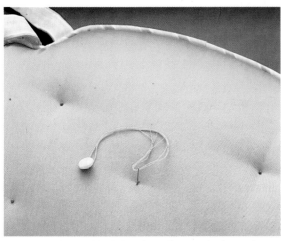

9 Insert the ends of the thread strands through the eye of a long needle. Insert needle through cushion to back side. Remove strands from needle; divide strands into two groups.

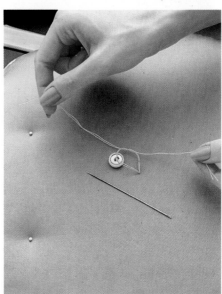

10 Thread second button on one group of threads; tie a single knot, using both thread groups; pull until buttons are tight against cushion, creating indentation. Wrap the thread two or three times around the button shank. Tie a double knot; trim thread tails.

BUTTONED PILLOWS

These easy-to-sew decorative pillows get added style from their interesting buttons. The buttoned envelope-style pillow is sewn from one rectangle and can be made either with a flange (middle) or without (left). The buttoned closure is centered on the pillow, horizontally or vertically.

The buttoned-end pillow (right) is made from two fabric rectangles and features buttoned flanges on both ends of the pillow. Buttons are also sewn to the back side of the flange to make the pillow attractive on both sides.

The fabric yardage requirements vary with the size of the pillow. It may be possible to cut the pillow rectangles on the crosswise grain, depending on the size of the rectangles and on the width and design of the fabric. Decorative shank buttons up to 1¼" (3.2 cm) in diameter are recommended for the buttoned pillows.

HOW TO SEW A BUTTONED ENVELOPE-STYLE PILLOW

MATERIALS

- Decorator fabric.
- Decorative buttons.
- Pillow form.
- Polyester fiberfill.

CUTTING DIRECTIONS

For a horizontal closure, cut one rectangle from fabric, with the length equal to two times the length of the pillow form plus 10" (25.5 cm) for the hems and overlap; for a flanged pillow, also add 8" (20.5 cm) for the flanges. The width of the rectangle is equal to the width of the pillow form plus 1" (2.5 cm) for seam allowances; for a flanged pillow, also add 4" (10 cm) for the flanges.

For a vertical closure, cut one rectangle from fabric, with the length equal to the length of the pillow form plus 1" (2.5 cm) for seam allowances; for a flanged pillow, also add 4" (10 cm) for the flanges. The width of the rectangle is equal to two times the width of the pillow form plus 10" (25.5 cm) for the hems and overlap; for a flanged pillow, also add 8" (20.5 cm) for the flanges.

1 Without flanges. Press under 2" (5 cm) twice to make double-fold hems on both ends of the rectangle, for the closure. Hand-stitch or machine-stitch in place.

2 Make the buttonholes on hem overlap as shown; space the buttonholes evenly between seam allowances and position them about ⅝" (1.5 cm) from folded edge.

3 Fold the fabric, right sides together, centering the double-fold hems; place the hem underlap for the buttons on top of hem overlap with buttonholes. Pin, matching the raw edges.

4 Stitch along the raw edges, using ½" (1.3 cm) seam allowances. Clip the corners diagonally. Turn pillow cover right side out; press.

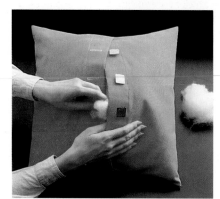

5 Stitch buttons on hem underlap. Insert pillow form; push polyester fiberfill into corners of pillow cover as necessary to fill out pillow. Button the pillow cover.

1 With flanges. Follow steps 1 to 4; in step 2, take into account a 2" (5 cm) flange depth and ½" (1.3 cm) seam allowances when determining the spacing between the buttonholes. Measure 2" (5 cm) from the edges of pillow cover to mark depth of flange on each side.

2 Pin layers together. Stitch on the marked lines, pivoting at corners to form the flange. Complete pillow as in step 5.

HOW TO SEW A BUTTONED-END PILLOW

MATERIALS

- Decorator fabric.
- Decorative buttons, two for each buttonhole.
- Pillow form.
- Polyester fiberfill.

CUTTING DIRECTIONS

Cut two rectangles from fabric, for the front and the back of the pillow, with the width of the rectangles on the crosswise grain. The width of the fabric rectangles is equal to the longest dimension of the pillow form plus 10" (25.5 cm) for the flanges and facings. The length of the fabric rectangles is equal to the shortest dimension of the pillow form plus 1" (2.5 cm) for seam allowances.

1 Place pillow front and pillow back right sides together. Stitch ½" (1.3 cm) seam on upper and lower edges; leave opening, centered on the lower edge, for inserting the pillow form. Press the seam allowances open.

2 Turn pillow cover right side out. Fold under 3" (7.5 cm) at ends; press lightly.

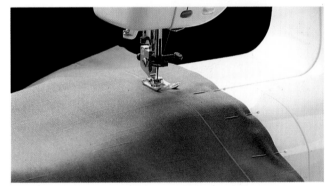

3 Align the folded edges at ends; pin. Stitch through all layers 2" (5 cm) from folded edges, to form flanges.

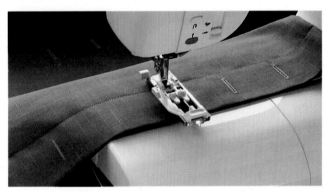

4 Mark desired placement for buttonholes; space evenly and center the width of the buttonholes on flanges as shown. Stitch buttonholes through all layers; cut open.

5 Hand-stitch two buttons together so the buttons face in opposite directions; do not cut thread. Insert buttons through a buttonhole so one button is exposed on each side of the flange; tack the buttons in place to prevent any shifting. Repeat for remaining buttons.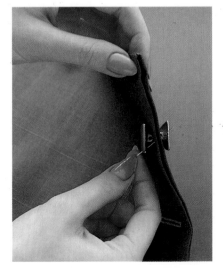

6 Insert pillow form; push polyester fiberfill into corners of pillow cover as necessary to fill out pillow. Pin opening closed, and slipstitch or edgestitch close to folded edge.

TIE-TAB PILLOWS

Tie-tab pillows are created by covering a knife-edge inner pillow with a pillowcase that has a tie-tab closure on one side. The tabs on the case can be tied in knots or bows, depending on the look desired. This pillow style provides an opportunity to combine coordinating fabrics, because the inner pillow is visible between the tie tabs along the closure side.

The number of tabs needed will vary with the size of the pillow. Two tabs are needed for each tie. Evenly space the tabs about 3" to 4" (7.5 to 10 cm) apart.

The instructions that follow are for a knife-edge inner pillow and a tie-tab pillowcase with tapered corners. Tapering the stitching at the corners eliminates dog-eared corners on the finished pillow. If you are making the inner pillow or the pillowcase from a plaid or striped fabric, you may prefer not to taper the corners.

MATERIALS

- Decorator fabric, for inner pillow, pillowcase, and tabs.
- Pillow form.
- Polyester fiberfill, for filling out corners.

CUTTING DIRECTIONS

For the knife-edge inner pillow, cut the pillow front and back 1" (2.5 cm) wider and longer than the pillow form.

For the pillowcase, cut the case front and back 1" (2.5 cm) wider and ½" (1.3 cm) longer than the pillow form. Also cut a facing strip 1½" (3.8 cm) wide, with the length equal to two times the width of the pillow form plus 1" (2.5 cm). For each tab, cut two 1¼" (3.2 cm) strips of fabric. For knotted tabs, cut the strips 8" (20.5 cm) long; for tabs tied into bows, cut the strips 12" (30.5 cm) long.

HOW TO SEW A KNIFE-EDGE PILLOW

1 Fold pillow front into fourths. For tapered corners, mark a point halfway between corner and fold on each open side. At corner, mark a point ⅜" (1 cm) from each raw edge.

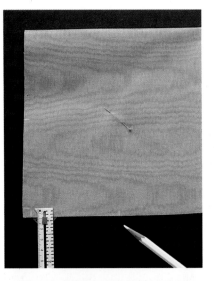

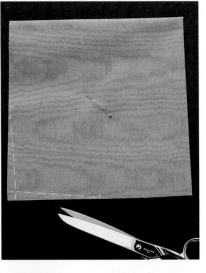

2 Mark lines, tapering from the raw edges at center marks to marks at corner. Cut along the marked lines.

3 Use pillow front as a pattern for cutting pillow back so that all corners are tapered. This will eliminate dog-eared corners on the finished pillow.

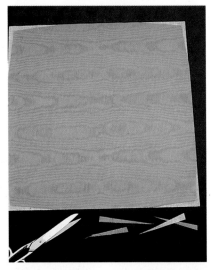

4 Pin the pillow front to pillow back, right sides together. Stitch a ½" (1.3 cm) seam, leaving opening on one side for turning and for inserting pillow form.

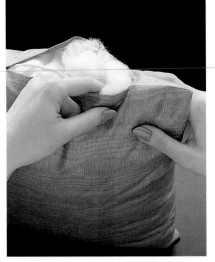

5 Turn pillow cover right side out, pulling out corners. Press under seam allowances at opening.

6 Insert pillow form; push fiberfill into the corners of the pillow as necessary to fill out pillow.

7 Pin opening closed; slipstitch or edgestitch close to folded edge.

HOW TO SEW A TIE-TAB PILLOWCASE

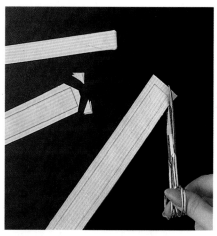

1 Fold pillowcase front in half. Mark and cut tapered corners at one end as in steps 1 and 2, opposite; do not taper corners at edge of case where the ties will be stitched. Use case front as a pattern for case back.

2 Pin case front to case back, right sides together. Stitch around sides, using a ½" (1.3 cm) seam allowance and leaving untapered edge unstitched; press seams open. Turn the case right side out, pulling out the corners.

3 Place two tab strips right sides together, matching the raw edges. Stitch ¼" (6 mm) seam around long sides and one end of tab. Repeat for remaining tabs. Trim corners, and turn the tabs right side out; press.

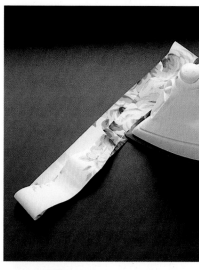

4 Pin tabs to right side of the case along unstitched edge, keeping the raw edges even and spacing the tabs evenly; position end tabs about 2½" (6.5 cm) from the seam.

5 Fold facing strip, right sides together, matching short ends; stitch ½" (1.3 cm) seam. Press the seam open. Press up ¼" (6 mm) along one edge of the facing strip.

6 Pin unpressed edge of facing strip to open edge of pillowcase, right sides together and raw edges even. Stitch ½" (1.3 cm) seam; trim the seam allowance. Press facing to the wrong side of the case.

7 Machine-stitch or hand-stitch facing in place. Insert pillow. Tie tabs into bows or knots.

MORE IDEAS
FOR PILLOWS

**Buttoned envelope-style
pillow** (page 105) has the
overlap positioned near one
side of the pillow for an
asymmetrical look.

**Buttoned-end and
tasseled pillows** are
grouped together for
impact. A variety of
buttons are used on the
buttoned-end pillow
(page 105) to give a
whimsical look. Ball
tassels embellish the
corners of the simple
knife-edge pillows
(page 109).

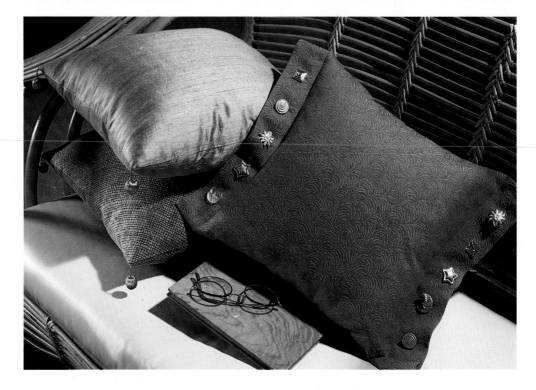

Tapestry pillow is framed with mitered border. The border is applied to the center panel as on pages 86 and 87.

Tufted pillow with welting showcases a large center button. The welting is applied to the knife-edge pillow as on page 90, and the center button is applied as on page 103.

Southwestern-style pillows are decorated with conchos and beads. Conchos with knotted leather strips are secured to the corners and center of a knife-edge pillow (page 109). Leather laces replace the fabric tabs on a tie-tab pillow (page 109).

LAMP SHADES

Make a customized lamp shade to coordinate with the decorating scheme of any room. Choose from either pleated or unpleated styles. Both styles can be made with either wallcovering or fabric. All versions use a purchased smooth lamp shade as a base.

For a pleated wallcovering shade, select a wallcovering or border that easily holds a crease, such as a paper-backed vinyl wallcovering. For an unpleated lamp shade from wallcovering, avoid using a wallcovering that has a striped or plaid pattern.

For a fabric-covered lamp shade, select a mediumweight fabric, such as decorator cotton or damask. Avoid using a fabric with a striped or plaid pattern for the unpleated fabric-covered lamp shade.

HOW TO MAKE A PATTERN FOR AN UNPLEATED LAMP SHADE

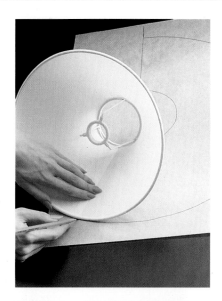

1 Mark a line, longer than the height of the lamp shade, on a large sheet of paper. Position lamp shade on paper, aligning seam of shade to the marked line. Roll lamp shade, and trace upper edge of shade to seam, using pencil; realign lamp shade seam with the marked line. Roll lamp shade, and trace lower edge of shade to seam.

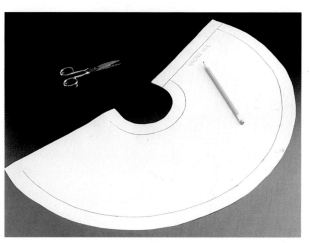

2 Cut out paper pattern, allowing 1" (2.5 cm) excess paper around all edges. Label the pattern for wrong side of shade cover.

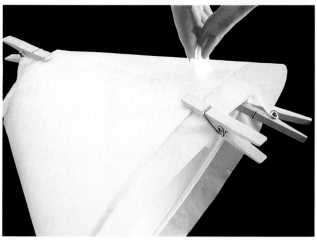

3 Position pattern on lamp shade, wrong side of pattern toward shade, aligning marked line to seam on shade; clamp, using clothespins. Tape ends together. Check fit of pattern, and redraw lines as necessary.

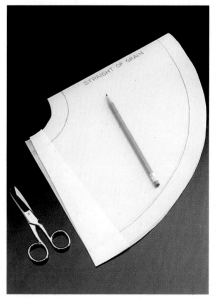

4 Remove the pattern; cut on straight line marked in step 1. Fold the pattern in half; crease. Mark crease for the lengthwise or crosswise direction of the wallcovering or fabric. Trim upper and lower edges of pattern, ⅝" (1.5 cm) from marked lines.

HOW TO MAKE
AN UNPLEATED WALLCOVERING LAMP SHADE

MATERIALS

- Wallcovering.
- Smooth plastic or paper lamp shade, for base.
- Border adhesive; sponge applicator.
- Narrow trim, such as gimp or braid.
- Thick craft glue.
- Clothespins; sponge.

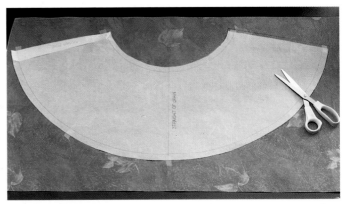

1 Make pattern (page 115). Position the pattern, wrong side down, on right side of wallcovering. Trace around pattern, adding ⅜" (1 cm) at one short end, for overlap. Cut on the lines marked on wallcovering.

2 Apply border adhesive to one-quarter of the lamp shade, starting about 3" (7.5 cm) from seam. Place cover on shade, aligning short end of cover with seam of shade; upper and lower edges will extend ⅝" (1.5 cm) beyond edge of shade. Smooth out any air bubbles or wrinkles in wallcovering.

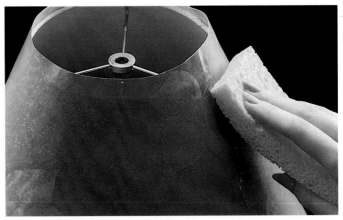

3 Continue to apply wallcovering to remainder of the lamp shade, working with one-quarter section at a time; overlap wallcovering at seam of shade. Remove any excess adhesive, using a damp sponge.

4 Make ½" (1.3 cm) clips, at ½" (1.3 cm) intervals, along upper edge of shade and at wire spokes. Fold wallcovering to inside of shade; secure, using border adhesive. Clamp the wallcovering in place as necessary with clothespins; allow to dry.

5 Make ½" (1.3 cm) clips, at ½" (1.3 cm) intervals, along lower edge of shade. Fold wallcovering to inside; secure with border adhesive, easing in extra fullness. Apply narrow trim to the upper and lower edges, to conceal edges of wallcovering; secure with thick craft glue.

HOW TO MAKE AN UNPLEATED FABRIC LAMP SHADE

MATERIALS

- Decorator fabric.
- Smooth plastic, paper, or fabric lamp shade, for base.
- Narrow trim, such as gimp or braid.
- Thick craft glue.
- Sponge applicator.
- Clothespins.

1 Make pattern (page 115). Position the pattern, wrong side down, on right side of the fabric, with center of pattern on the lengthwise or crosswise grain of fabric. Cut fabric, adding ⅜" (1 cm) at one short end for overlap.

2 Pour craft glue into bowl; dilute with water to creamy consistency. Apply the fabric to the shade as in step 2, opposite, using craft glue instead of the border adhesive. Take care not to stretch fabric on the bias.

3 Continue to apply fabric to remainder of shade, applying glue to one-quarter of shade at a time; take care not to stretch fabric on the bias.

4 Seal raw edges at back of shade with diluted craft glue. Complete shade as in steps 4 and 5, opposite, substituting craft glue for the border adhesive.

HOW TO MAKE A PLEATED WALLCOVERING LAMP SHADE

MATERIALS

- Wallcovering or wallcovering border, about ¾" (2 cm) taller than height of lamp shade.
- Smooth plastic or paper lamp shade, for base.
- Thick craft glue or hot glue gun and glue sticks.

- Transparent ruler.
- Soft elastic, about 1" (2.5 cm) wide, optional.
- String; plastic-coated paper clips.

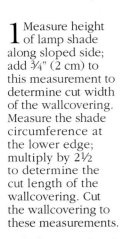

1 Measure height of lamp shade along sloped side; add ¾" (2 cm) to this measurement to determine cut width of the wallcovering. Measure the shade circumference at the lower edge; multiply by 2½ to determine the cut length of the wallcovering. Cut the wallcovering to these measurements.

2 Mark a light pencil line on the wrong side of the wallcovering, parallel to and 1" (2.5 cm) from upper long edge of strip. Repeat at lower edge. Mark pleat lines within marked lines, spaced 1½" (3.8 cm) apart and parallel to the short edges.

3 Fold wallcovering on the pleat lines, creasing sharply. Align adjacent pleat lines, and crease to fold crisp ¾" (2 cm) accordion pleats.

4 Overlap short ends of the pleated wallcovering; trim excess wallcovering. Divide pleated wallcovering and shade into fourths at upper edges; mark, using paper clips.

5 Secure pleated wallcovering into tightly folded bundle, using string; cushion the bundle with narrow strips of wallcovering to prevent marking the wallcovering. Set aside for several hours to set pleats.

6 Overlap the short ends of the pleated wallcovering, and secure, using thick craft glue; allow to dry.

7 Position the pleated wallcovering over the lamp shade, matching marks. Adjust pleats so they are even and extend about ½" (1.3 cm) above shade. Elastic, cut to fit around upper and lower edges of shade, may help to control fullness while position of pleats is adjusted.

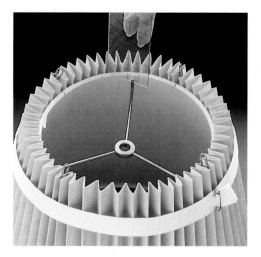

8 Secure pleated wallcovering to lamp shade at upper and lower edges, using thick craft glue or hot glue. Allow to dry.

HOW TO MAKE A PLEATED FABRIC LAMP SHADE

MATERIALS

- Lightweight to mediumweight fabric; amount varies, depending on size of lamp shade.
- Fabric stiffener; sponge applicator.
- Smooth plastic, paper, or fabric lamp shade, for base.

- Soft elastic, about 1" (2.5 cm) wide, optional.
- String; plastic-coated paper clips.
- Thick craft glue, or hot glue gun and glue sticks.

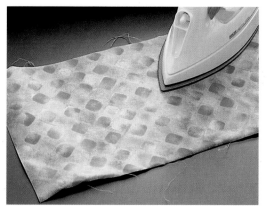

1 Measure lamp shade and cut the fabric as in step 1, opposite; add ¼" (6 mm) to height to allow for fabric shrinkage.

2 Cover work surface with plastic. Place fabric strip wrong side up, over plastic. Apply fabric stiffener to wrong side of fabric, using a sponge applicator; brush the stiffener from center to edges of fabric. Turn fabric right side up on plastic, keeping fabric flat and straight; allow to dry.

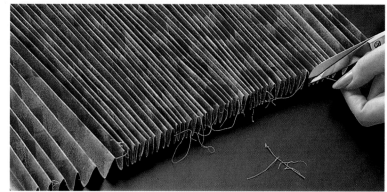

3 Press fabric on right side, using warm, dry iron; allow to cool.

4 Mark and pleat the fabric as in steps 2 and 3, opposite. Trim any threads at edges of fabric. Complete the shade as in steps 4 to 8, opposite.

MORE IDEAS FOR LAMP SHADES

Gimp trim *(left) is glued to the lower edge of a pleated wallcovering lamp shade.*

Braid trim *(below) embellishes the lower edge of an unpleated fabric-covered lamp shade.*

Wallcovering cutouts *(page 20) are used to embellish the unpleated wallcovering lamp shade at left.*

Border edging strip *is applied to the upper and lower edges of a pleated wallcovering lamp shade.*

Grouped pleats *create an interesting effect on a pleated fabric lamp shade. Glue three pleats together and alternate with single pleats for a distinctive look.*

FABRIC-COVERED PICTURE FRAMES

Create custom picture frames using fabrics that coordinate with your decorating scheme. Picture frames are an inexpensive way to introduce luxurious fabrics, such as silks, damasks, and tapestries. Embellish the frames, if desired, with trims, charms, or appliqués.

For best results, use firmly woven lightweight to mediumweight fabrics. If you are using a heavier fabric, reduce bulk by covering the frame back and the stand with a lightweight fabric. Lightly pad the frame, if desired, using polyester fleece.

MATERIALS

- Fabric.
- Polyester fleece, optional.
- Heavy cardboard, such as mat board or illustration board; precut mats may be used for the frame front.
- Clear acetate sheet, optional.
- Fabric glue, diluted slightly with water for easier spreading.
- Flat paintbrush or sponge applicator for applying glue.
- Aerosol adhesive intended for fabric use.
- Hot glue gun and glue sticks.

CUTTING DIRECTIONS

Determine the desired size of the frame and the frame opening; the opening should be slightly smaller than the photograph or picture. Mark these dimensions on the cardboard for the frame front. Mark the frame back on the cardboard ½" (1.3 cm) narrower and shorter than the frame front. Make the frame stand, if desired, as on page 124, steps 1 and 2, cutting the pieces for the frame stand with a mat knife and a straightedge. When cutting with a mat knife, it is better to use a few medium-pressure cuts than one heavy cut. Cut a clear acetate sheet, if desired, to the size of the photograph or picture.

HOW TO MAKE A FABRIC PICTURE FRAME

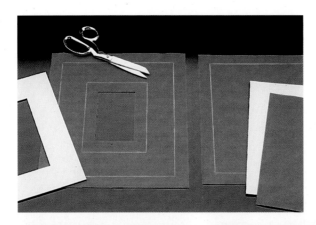

1 Position the frame front on wrong side of fabric; trace around frame and opening, using a pencil or chalk. Cut fabric 1" (2.5 cm) outside marked lines. Position frame back on wrong side of fabric, and trace around it; cut 1" (2.5 cm) outside the marked lines. Trace a second back piece; cut ⅛" (3 mm) inside marked lines.

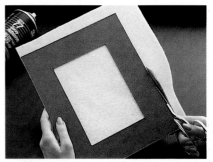

2 Apply fleece, if desired, to frame front, using aerosol adhesive; trim even with edges of cardboard.

3 Center frame front, fleece side down, on wrong side of the fabric for frame front; clip fabric at corners of frame opening to within a scant ⅛" (3 mm) of cardboard. Using diluted fabric glue, secure fabric to cardboard around the opening, gluing alternating sides.

4 Apply glue at one outer corner and along edges to center of adjacent sides. Wrap fabric firmly around edge of frame, pinching fabric together at corner as shown. Repeat for the remaining sides and corners.

5 Fold excess fabric at corners flat; secure with diluted fabric glue.

6 Apply smaller piece of fabric to frame back, using aerosol adhesive. Center frame back, fabric side up, on the wrong side of remaining fabric piece; secure with aerosol adhesive. Wrap and glue sides as for frame front. Seal raw edges of fabric with diluted fabric glue; this is inside of frame back.

(Continued)

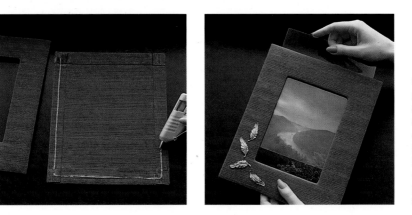

7 Apply hot glue to the inside of frame back along three edges; center the frame back on the frame front, and secure. One side of the frame is left open for inserting a photograph or a picture.

8 Make and attach frame stand (below), if desired. Attach embellishments as desired, securing them with glue. Insert photograph or picture and protective clear acetate sheet.

HOW TO MAKE A FRAME STAND

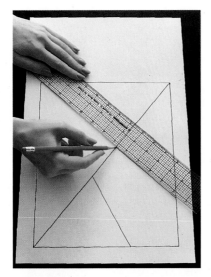

1 Mark the dimensions of frame on paper; divide rectangle in half diagonally. Measuring from the lower corner, mark point on each side of corner a distance equal to about one-third the width of the frame. Align a straightedge with one point and opposite corner; mark line from the point to diagonal marked line. Repeat for remaining point.

2 Cut out the frame stand pattern. Position on cardboard; trace. Cut out frame stand. Lightly score cardboard ½" (1.3 cm) from upper edge, using straightedge and mat knife; do not cut through cardboard. Flip stand over and gently crease cardboard along scored line as shown.

3 Position stand on wrong side of fabric, scored side up; trace. Cut ½" (1.3 cm) outside marked lines. Turn stand over and repeat to cut second piece, cutting ⅛" (3 mm) inside marked lines; this is lining piece.

4 Center stand, scored side up, on wrong side of larger fabric piece. Using diluted glue and brush, apply glue to the edges of fabric, and wrap around the edges of stand, clipping fabric at corners. Secure lining piece, centered, using aerosol adhesive. Seal the raw edges of fabric with diluted fabric glue.

5 Apply hot glue to lining side of frame stand above scored line. Secure the stand to the back of the frame, matching outer edges at the corner of the frame.

Brass wire *is wrapped around the corners of a fabric-covered frame for embellishment. The wire is applied before the back is secured in place.*

Wallcovering cutouts *embellish an acrylic frame. The wallcovering is applied using border adhesive.*

Wallcovering border *is used to trim a wooden frame. The mitered border is applied as on page 13.*

Trio of frames *is hinged by inserting ribbon between the frame fronts and backs. A ⅛" (3 mm) space is allowed between the frames to allow for folding. No frame stands are needed for hinged frames.*

INDEX

CREDITS

President: Iain Macfarlane

DECORATING WITH FABRIC
& WALLCOVERING
Created by: The Editors of
Creative Publishing international, Inc.

Books available in this series:
Bedroom Decorating, Creative Window
Treatments, Decorating for Christmas,
Decorating the Living Room, Creative
Accessories for the Home, Decorating
with Silk & Dried Flowers, Decorating
the Kitchen, Decorative Painting,
Kitchen & Bathroom Ideas, Decorating
Your Home for Christmas, Decorating
for Dining & Entertaining, Decorating
with Fabric & Wallcovering,
Decorating the Bathroom, Decorating
with Great Finds, Affordable
Decorating, Picture-Perfect Walls, More
Creative Window Treatments, Outdoor
Decor, The Gift of Christmas, Home
Accents in a Flash, Painted Illusions,
Halloween Decorating, 'Tis the Season

Group Executive Editor: Zoe A. Graul
Senior Technical Director: Rita C. Arndt
Technical Director: Dawn M. Anderson
Senior Project Manager: Kristen Olson
Assistant Project Manager: Elaine
 Johnson
Art Director: Mark Jacobson
Writer: Dawn M. Anderson
Editor: Janice Cauley

Researcher/Designer: Michael Basler
Researcher: Lori Ritter
Sample Supervisor: Carol Olson
Senior Technical Photo Stylist: Bridget
 Haugh
Technical Photo Stylists: Susan Pasqual,
 Nancy Sundeen
Styling Director: Bobbette Destiche
Crafts Stylist: Joanne Wawra
Prop Assistant/Shopper: Margo Morris
Artisans: Arlene Dohrman, Sharon
 Ecklund, Corliss Forstrom, Phyllis
 Galbraith, Valerie Kraker, Kristi Kuhnau,
 Virginia Mateen, Carol Pilot, Nancy
 Sundeen
Vice President of Development Planning
 & Production: Jim Bindas
Director of Photography: Mike Parker
Creative Photo Coordinator: Cathleen
 Shannon
Studio Manager: Marcia Chambers
Lead Photographer: Stuart Block
Photographers: Rebecca Hawthorne,
 Kevin Hedden, Mike Hehner, Rex
 Irmen, William Lindner, Mark
 Macemon, Paul Najlis, Charles
 Nields, Mike Parker, Robert Powers
Contributing Photographers: Kim Bailey,
 Doug Cummelin, Mette Nielsen, Brad
 Parker, Steve Smith
Production Manager: Laurie Gilbert
Senior Desktop Publishing Specialist:
 Joe Fahey
Production Staff: Deborah Eagle, Kevin
 Hedden, Mike Hehner, Jeff Hickman,
 Laurie Kristensen, Jeanette Moss,
 Michelle Peterson, Robert Powers,
 Mike Schauer, Kay Wethern, Nik
 Wogstad

Shop Supervisor: Phil Juntti
Scenic Carpenters: Rob Johnstone, John
 Nadeau, Mike Peterson
Consultants: Ray Arndt, Sr., Lana
 Bennett, Joyce Eide, Amy Engman,
 Constance Erickson, Lindsey Peterson,
 Kay Sanders
Contributors: Conso Products Company;
 Dritz Corporation; EZ International;
 Fairfield Processing Corporation;
 Graber Industries, Inc.; Kirsch; Putnam
 Company, Inc.; Swiss-Metrosene, Inc.;
 Waverly, Division of F. Schumacher &
 Company
Printed on American paper by:
 R. R. Donnelley & Sons Co.
03 02 01 00 99 / 6 5 4 3 2

Creative Publishing international, Inc.
offers a variety of how-to books. For
information write:
 Creative Publishing international, Inc.
 Subscriber Books
 5900 Green Oak Drive
 Minnetonka, MN 55343